53. School Days

Back at school, Andy was still not speaking to me. After another couple of "I am so sorry"s, Charlotte, Devon, and I were back sitting together at lunch, but a repeat invitation for a sleepover was not happening anytime soon. At least I had someone to sit with.

Friday came and I gave Mr. J my new outline. I wanted to write about friendship and family, but since I could only choose one, I decided to write about Grammy and how she was there for me.

Nate took the news about doing his own homework well, grunting, "Hmmpf, I figured you would bail on me." The jury was still out on whether he needed surgery. All weekend, Nate kept making loud banging noises with the cast and the crutches. I guess that he needs to keep getting all the attention somehow.

Connie called me to thank me for my letter and ask what our plans were for the holidays. She and her mom were thinking of taking a trip to Chicago! That was unexpected and kind of weird. If not the holidays, then in the spring. Her brother was thinking of applying to Northwestern University, where there was some sort of family connection.

About another week and a half later, I could feel things getting better with Andy. He waited for me to go to lunch, and we talked for the first time since our essay argument.

"Andy, I apologize for wanting to write about your adoption. I know now that is your story to tell. I was going to change your name in the story, but I totally understand."

"Yeah, I've been thinking about everything, and I know you cared enough to help me." He paused, then said, "My mom reached out to Angela and she'd like to meet me."

"Oh, wow. That's great news."

"I had just talked myself into believing that she didn't want me. It was my mom and dad that were more interested in a private adoption. Mom showed me the pictures she has been emailing to Angela for years now. I couldn't believe it. Angela said she loved seeing how I was growing up. We're meeting closer to Christmas."

"That's the best news I have heard in forever, Andy. Congrats. I am now declaring KISSS a success!"

Andy threw back his head and laughed with his mouth wide open. It reminded me of Connie for a second. Then he said, "Oh, I forgot to tell you the weirdest thing. When I was talking to my mom about Angela, she said don't forget that I need to give Angela grace, who had to make some hard decisions because of her family. I guess there was a bunch of other stuff going on that I'll find out later. Then Mom also asked me to give her and Dad grace because they were trying to do what they thought was best. I just thought it was kind of weird that everyone was saying the same thing. That's why today, I had to talk to you."

With that, Andy stood up and folded his hands like he was praying. "And Grace, I give you grace, and hope that you give the same to me. Can we be friends again?"

"Yes, for sure." I laughed.

"Will you stick around for part two, when I meet Angela in person? She looks very nice from the pictures I've seen, but I am nervous about meeting face to face. Do you think she'll like me?"

I don't know why but I grabbed Andy's hand, then gave him a hug. He acted surprised, so I said quickly, "She will love you … c'mon, we have to get to class."

54. Family

We rode the bus home together that day and, as it pulled away, I waved to Andy until I couldn't see him anymore.

Once inside, I heard that familiar voice. "Grammy!" I yelled and ran to give her a hug.

"When I got your letter, I just had to see you. Are things getting better?"

"Yes, Andy is talking to me again." Everything else came out in a jumbled rush and I couldn't stop talking … and then I was crying.

"It's okay, honey." Grammy smoothed my hair and kissed my cheek. It was wonderful to see her again.

Grammy and I smiled at each other. I could feel the huge ring as I held her hand. And then almost reading my thoughts Grammy said, "Not pushing up daisies anytime soon. I am always here for you."

"Grace, will you set the table?" Mom asked from the kitchen. I could see she was getting one of

Grammy's favorite dinners together—some kind of stir-fry beef thing with noodles that I could never remember the name of. On the way to the kitchen, I saw the mail on the table in the hallway and couldn't believe my eyes. An envelope was addressed to me with Mildred's name clear as day in the return address space!

Mildred outdid herself with stationery that was impossible to miss. Two purple and pink tulips were printed in the left corner of the envelope, which was tied with a green ribbon that went around the back. The return address said Mildred, Chicago, IL.

OMG. Mildred wrote back to me! I thought she wasn't allowed to, or her senior center said it was against the rules. Who cared? I shoved the letter in my pocket and set the table, almost throwing the dishes and silverware in place.

"Where's the fire?" Mom said.

"Sorry, I'm going upstairs to do a bit of homework before dinner."

"Did you see you got a letter in the mail? Who's Mildred?"

"She's just a friend."

"I didn't know you had any letter writing friends in Chicago."

"It's kind of a long story that I'll have to tell you later."

"Okay, dinner is at six."

Upstairs, I grabbed my flashlight and crawled under the quilt. Inside the envelope was a white single sheet of paper with the same purple and pink tulips at the bottom of the page tied with a green ribbon. I sniffed it. If there was a special Mildred scent, I couldn't detect it.

Dear Grace,

First, thank you for writing to me. It's rare for a young girl to take the time to write to a senior, so I can tell you have a good heart and a generous spirit.

It was oodles of fun for me to see all the things that you are doing at school to keep busy. Did you like horseback riding? Was it difficult to get used to a new school? It sounded like you were making friends.

That is the main reason that I am writing to you. I know friendships are very important at your age. It seemed like you were worried about the kids at school not liking you or you were finding it difficult to make friends.

Grace, your road to confidence in making friends starts with you. When we don't like ourselves, we don't find ourselves worthy of friends. Only when we are happy with ourselves can we go after the things that bring us joy. Your horseback riding lessons sound like the beginning of that journey.

How you feel about yourself, your thoughts, and feelings are changing all the time. Difficult life experiences can certainly affect those feelings. Grace, you are enough. You are worthy of friends.

Know that you are not alone in this life. Your parents and teachers can help.

I hope you continue to find the things that bring you happiness but find that happiness in yourself first.

Good luck with more KISSS and all the fun things in life.

Your favorite senior,

Mildred

55. The Family Chain Stitch

Grammy gushed over dinner and Mom beamed. I couldn't stop thinking about Mildred and her letter. Grammy was the ideal person that Mildred was talking about. She always seemed perfectly happy and content. Her life back in Pennsylvania suited her fine. She would never move to Chicago just to be with us because she had friends, maybe even a boyfriend. That could be why I heard her whispering with Mom.

    Dad gave everyone an update about work. Everything seemed to be going well. Mom loved her job at the library. Nate even broke away from video games to sit with Grammy before dinner. Surprising even himself, he talked about a book report he was writing. All my worries were for nothing. Grammy asked him about his plan B if football didn't work out, which was kind of an off-limits subject in our house.

"I don't know," came the reply. Was that the first time it crossed his mind? Grammy was good at stuff like that … saying things that needed to be said.

I had a surprise for Grammy after dinner and I couldn't wait. But first, Mom needed our help with the dishes.

"How's Charlotte?" Mom asked. "Why don't you invite her and Devon to sleep here one weekend?"

Things had been a bit upside down at the house for a while, and I hadn't even thought of that. "Oh, that's a great idea." Maybe Mildred was right. I had to be happy first, doing the things that were good for me. It felt good to be the one starting the friendship.

After dinner in her room, Grammy started to pull out all the yarn and crochet hooks. When she was all propped up with a pillow and blankets, I put my surprise chain stitch in her lap. Grammy smiled. "Oh my, look at that," she said, examining my work under the light from the bedside table. "You have picked it up quite fast. How did you do it?"

"YouTube," I said. "You can learn anything in a video." We both laughed like that was the funniest thing in the world.

"It looks lovely, Grace. You are now ready to graduate and move to a real scarf. What are you thinking about colors? It may be a bit close for

Christmas presents, but we can try. Let's make a list and we'll go out while I'm here to get more yarn."

"I'll get a pen and paper for our list. Maybe the yarn shop will be having a sale."

I left everything on the bed and started digging in Grammy's carry on.

"Oh no, not in there, Gracie." Grammy held her hand out to stop me.

Too late. My hands found paper and a pen at the bottom of the bag. But when I looked down at the paper, I was confused. In my hand, I held a couple of sheets of white paper with pink and purple tulips in the corner. It was the exact same paper that Mildred used to write to me!

Wait, did Mildred actually write to me?

Grammy's face told the story.

"Gracie, when I was here last, you were extremely sad about your friendship situation. You fell asleep at your desk, and I read your letter to Mildred. I know I shouldn't have."

I couldn't believe what I was hearing and sat down at the edge of the bed when Grammy continued.

"Then I got your last letter about your trouble with Andy, and you were beyond distraught. I just wanted to tell you that everything would be okay, and anyone would be very lucky to have you as a friend."

"But Mildred's letter is from Chicago. You don't live in Chicago."

"Yes, I know. Your mom agreed to help me. I sent the letter to your mom who mailed it from Chicago. You know her, we made a deal. I'd slow down with my lottery obsession and she'd help with my secret mission."

Just then, Mom came into the room and sat with me on the bed. "Gracie, we both love you very much and want you to know that whatever you want to do with horses, with friends, with family … we support you one hundred percent."

"That goes for me too," Dad piped in, sticking his head in the room. "We know Nate is a lot, and I don't just mean body odor and farts."

"Dad, please." I was suddenly embarrassed, but not enough to stop smiling. My family was awesome. And … I loved my friends. I thought about everything that happened and suddenly was excited and happy to tell Andy, Charlotte, and most of all Connie. To celebrate, I squeezed Lily and laughed as loud as I could.

Later that night, instead of going straight to my room, I knocked on Nate's door first. Maybe it was time to tell him that I loved him, too. But I still wasn't going to do his homework for him.

After that, I would write a letter to Mildred to tell her that I am getting the hang of friendship.

I could really get used to this!

Find yourself ... find a friend!

Finding a friend can be tough.
A shot of confidence can help!

See our **ACT FUNSheets** (and more)
for **AFFIRMATIONS** to jump start
your self-assuredness

For **FUNSheets** and other goodies,
visit amdidio.com

Reviews are really important to me.

They help other readers and warm my heart!

*Take a moment to leave
a review filled with stars ...*

For more, visit amdidio.com

Thank You!

GRACE'S WRITE TIME

Anna Maria DiDio

Copyright © 2024 Anna Maria DiDio

All rights reserved. No part of this book may be reproduced, distributed, or transmitted in any form or by any means, electronic or mechanical, including photocopying and recording, without the prior written permission from the publisher, except in the case of brief quotations embodied in a book review and certain other non-commercial uses permitted by copyright law.

ISBN-13: 978-1-7377035-4-9

This is a work of fiction. Names, characters, places, and incidents are the product of the author's imagination.

Love At The Border Publishing, Philadelphia, PA
First Print Edition 2024

Published in the United States of America.

Cover illustration by Amalia Tucci, cover graphic art by Katie Lee Grosskoff.

For more information, visit the author's website: www.amdidio.com

*For all adoptees who want
to know their story …*

Chapters ...

1. The News 1
2. The Job of Parents 5
3. Writing Letters 9
4. The Jobs of Parents 15
5. Betty Can Help a Little 17
6. Goodbye Connie, Hello Chicago 21
7. Moving 29
8. Our New House 33
9. New But Thinking of Old 35
10. A New School 39
11. A Letter 43
12. New School New Friends 47
13. Mr. J 51
14. Nate 55
15. Social Media 59
16. Friday Night Football 61
17. Letters to the Rescue 65
18. Back at School Back at Home 69
19. Exercise Is Good for Me 73
20. Andy 79
21. Horseback Riding Lessons 83
22. Andy Has a Question 87

23. Grammy	93
24. Football	99
25. Chicago Shopping	103
26. Yarn	109
27. Goodnight Mildred	113
28. Church	115
29. Grammy Love	117
30. Andy Is Waiting	121
31. Mr. J's Essay Contest	125
32. Two Heads are Better Than One	129
33. Mildred Learns About KISSS	135
34. Tied to Family	137
35. My First Lesson	141
36. Girlfriends	147
37. Connie	151
38. The Adoption Box	153
39. Hope on a Post-It Note	159
40. Letter to Grammy	163
41. Sunday–Not in Church	165
42. Friendship is Complicated	167
43. The Football and Adoption Wound	173
44. Football Friday	177
45. The Plan	181

46. Chicago 185
47. Caught KISSSing 191
48. From Bad to Worse 195
49. Paper and Pen 201
50. Back at School 207
51. Even Andy 211
52. Grammy Cares 217
53. School Days 219
54. Family 223
55. The Family Chain Stitch 227

1. The News

It was the crunching that gave me away. I was in my usual after-school hideout eating Lucky Charms cereal when my brother Nate yanked the covers off of my head.

"I found her!" he announced, then said to me without looking, "Come downstairs, dingus." Nate paused at the door of my room. "I knew you'd be in there ... family meeting." He was not phased at all by my hateful glare. After all, he was the "do no wrong" child, perfect in every way.

I turned off my flashlight and stuck out my tongue behind his back. What was so important that he had to interrupt my journey into the magical world of *Alice in Wonderland*. I was reading it for the third time because the fantastical trek through the forest never disappoints. After school I try to block out the day under a mountain of fluffy pillows and fleece blankets on my bed. The pink and blue afghan baby blanket that Grammy Ollie made warms me to my toes, even if I'm now too old for a blankie.

"Gracie, where are you? Grace Elizabeth Mackenzie, come down here for a few minutes," my mother shouted from the living room. "We have some news to tell you."

News? Is that why Dad was home at three o'clock in the afternoon and not his usual six o'clock or seven? I noticed that things had been a bit weird lately. Last night my parents stopped talking as soon as I came into the room and gave each other a look like they just swallowed something gross.

Also, my mom has started biting her nails again. She told me it was a bad habit from when she was first married. To break her "pattern of self-destructive behavior," as she called it, Mom tried manicures in all shades of pretty colors. Perfectly Pink was her favorite. But that didn't seem to work, and she ended up biting off or scraping the polish clean. Then she tried some sort of icky solution from the drugstore. It smelled bad, but that didn't stop her either.

I am going into seventh grade and have accepted my parents as flawed human beings.

For our family meeting, Nate slouched on the couch, not a care in the world, gray flannel plaid shirt under his favorite black hoodie. His thick head of dark brown hair was a carefree mess, his blue eyes focused on a baseball that he was tossing up and down.

Dad was preoccupied on his phone in the corner of the room. Hunched over and intense, he struggled to pull off his tie and wriggle out of his jacket as he spoke quietly. What was that all about?

"Nate, stop that." Mom was perched on the edge of her favorite chair, which was covered in a fabric of faded roses. She had stayed home from school. I could tell by her mom jeans and sweatshirt. Why didn't I get my mom's type of hair? She never does much maintenance and it always looks nice. My mousy brown hair always seems to be frizzy. On the plus side, we are both tall and thin with freckled faces to match.

I sat teetered on the arm of the sofa next to Nate. Normally Mom wouldn't let me sit there, but she was distracted.

"What's the big news?" I blurted.

"We're moving!" my mom said a little too loudly.

"Yes!" Nate yelled and pumped his fist, knocking me off the edge of the couch and onto the floor. Just like that, no introduction, and no warning—my life was now over.

2. The Job of Parents

I stayed on the floor for a minute while Mom rambled on about Dad's new job and our "exciting adventure."

"What? We're moving? Why?" I got up to rub my knee.

"Well …" Mom paused dramatically. "Your dad has just been hired by a large advertising agency in Chicago!" She waited for some kind of reaction. Dad was still absorbed with something riveting on his phone.

"But I like where we live now. I thought Dad loved his job at the ad agency in Philadelphia."

"Chicago is a bigger sales area than the one he has here in Pennsylvania. The new agency has brands that you've heard of. It's a tremendous opportunity for him. Plus, now you can go to a much more progressive school. The Brookhaven school district there is very well-known."

Progressive? Well-known to who? Or is it whom? Mom was always frustrated with our tiny town school. She constantly complained that they were not using the "latest" textbooks, technology or resources.

My mom was the best librarian ever, but she never let us forget that we lived in the smallest Pennsylvania school district. We barely had enough girls for a middle school field hockey team (I should know. My parents made me play. "Athletic activity is SO good for you," they said). There were no SMART Boards in our classrooms. At graduation, some of the seniors had to come off the stage to play in the band. But was bigger always better?

"Besides," Mom said, "Nate will be able to plan for a future in football. With his experience, the coach thinks Nate could easily make varsity at his new school where he could be scouted for a football scholarship."

I turned to Nate. "You knew?"

"Sure, this is the best news ever for me."

Nate's favorite movie was Invincible, a true story about a professional football player who was a walk-on for the Philadelphia Eagles and went on to become a local and NFL legend. He's got big dreams, I'll give him that.

Nate flashed his cocky as all-get-out look and started tossing the baseball up and down again. Sometimes he could be such a jerk. I legit hated him for a minute (again).

3. Writing Letters

There is a ginormous difference between being alone and being lonely.

I like being alone sometimes, but being lonely is a different feeling altogether. It's like when we are at the beach, and I duck under a wave. No one sees me as I'm being pulled under. I have disappeared like a David Copperfield vanishing act, water swirling above me. My family is clueless.

I love my parents, but sometimes I wonder what they see when they finally do look at me. I am not a star athlete or remotely attractive. My crazy curly hair, glasses "for distance," and sticks for arms and legs take care of that. And now, even my wonderful report cards are expected.

Sometimes, I want to bounce up and down and scream, "Look at me, look at me!"

Nate is the star of this family. He is a super athlete, but best at football and on the varsity squad at our high school. It's a short roster because our school is adorably small, but still, he's played in every single game. I guess that's a big deal. He's charming to other people, and smart, but doesn't care too much for schoolwork. That's where I come in. School is where I shine. The only time Nate speaks to me is to get my help to write a book report, essay, or pretty much any other written homework.

The best medicine for my loneliness is writing letters. Writing connects me to someone in a kind of special, almost magical way. When I share my thoughts, feelings, or anything on paper, it's like I am speaking to another person without having to look at them. They're seeing me, but I'm not there.

I begin with new stationery out of the box, nice and crisp. Nothing says "fresh start" like a clean sheet of writing paper. Currently, my latest letter writing efforts are directed to old ladies in nursing homes, or "community dwelling" adults, as they are called. It makes me feel better to say things to them that I am unable to say to the actual older people in my life … like my parents.

There are lots of websites where anyone can sign up to send cards or letters to rando old people. I know because I have searched them all. There are even detailed instructions about how to write a letter in case you don't know what you're doing.

Here's some advice from a blog post titled You Can Make An Elder Smile Today…

Letters must be "legible," meaning LARGE print as who knows what their eyesight is like. Handwritten cards are preferred, with a big plus for Magic Marker text or colorful drawings or stickers. Oh, and no kidding here, absolutely no glitter is permitted. That must get in their eyes or stick to their skin, I guess.

Websites with names like Elder Horizons and Love for Seniors remind pen pals to be kind and thoughtful, but please do not expect a letter back. Okay—I read you loud and clear. These folks are already on the "back nine" of life. My family loves to talk in sports lingo—more on that later.

Feel free to add fun photos or even drawings or homemade crossword puzzles. An artist, I'm not, so I will be sticking to words.

Today I picked a senior named Betty who lives in Akron, Ohio. Her husband of forty years recently passed away. The last years were difficult due to his dementia. My letter was short because I had some stickers and got creative with a pastel marker set that I got for Christmas.

Dear Betty,

Hello and how are you? I found your information on the Elder Horizons website and decided to write.

You must have the most awesome memories from forty years with your husband. I have only lived twelve years with my brother, and he gets more annoying every day. I cannot imagine living that long with him. Thankfully, I probably won't have to. What was your favorite memory, if you only had to name one? I know that life can be lonely at times. I have experienced times when I needed to talk to someone and didn't know what to do.

Do you like where you are living now? Do you have friends there?

You don't have to write back but please know that I am thinking about you. There are people in the world that care about you.

Hugs,
Grace Elizabeth

It's important to remind old people about the wonderful things from their lives. Memories are precious.

Grace's Write Time

    I write to my Grammy Ollie occasionally, but she is not the letter writing type. When I think about my own family, I wonder where I came from.

4. The Jobs of Parents

Dad walked past my room still texting, but stuck his head in saying, "Peanut, this will be good for you too. Before you know it, you'll be looking at colleges."

It annoyed me that Dad used his nickname for me. Like he thought that somehow it was going to smooth things over and make me feel better. I had grown far beyond the "peanut" stage. In fact, I have not stopped growing. It's embarrassing to be as tall as your father in sixth grade. Dad didn't seem to mind though.

He tried to smile reassuringly at me, but I turned away … then immediately felt bad and turned back. Dad ran a hand through his salt and pepper hair. He'd been wearing his glasses a lot lately, which added to his nerd factor plus made his hazel eyes looked tired. Today he wore a smart casual button-down, light blue shirt, dark tie and gray pants. The texting resumed at a ferocious pace. What was that about?

"So, this is all arranged?" I squeaked.

"Uh huh," Dad kind of grunted, "You will definitely be excited once we get there, you'll see."

No, I didn't see at all. Everyone in my family had a chance to say something about this move except me. My family is full of expert talkers. There isn't a person that my dad could not sell something to, or my mom could not outtalk about her favorite book. My brother could strike up a bromance with anyone within one-hundred yards of a football field, if I am being honest.

In every conversation, I am the DL: designated listener. No wonder no one cares what I think—they never get to hear it!

The conversation with Dad was over, and I crawled under my blanket hut to steam about being left out of the family loop. Nate would get the football scholarship that has been part of his plan forever. Mom seemed giddy at the thought of moving into a Chicago "big league" library. Clearly Dad had not been happy with his career path, but now finally landed his dream job. I was thrilled for him, really I was.

But the thought of starting over somewhere made me feel sick.

5. Betty Can Help a Little

When I'm angry or have something to say, I am not very good at saying it. It's not a stutter. It's nothing. I'm truly an expert at avoiding talking. My tongue gets twisted the minute I open my mouth. When I am writing or reading, my brain relaxes and it all seems so uncomplicated and effortless. But the minute I want to talk—and I really do want to sometimes—I just can't.

Sometimes I write down exactly what people say to me. It's like a calm pill or mood booster shot in the arm. The act of writing gives something back to me: a burst of confidence, a belief in myself. I don't know exactly how it works, and it only lasts for a moment. How can I make it stick?

The other day Nate laughed. "Hey Beanpole, do you realize that you are growing up, but not out … if you know what I mean." Lifting weights in the garage in front of a recently installed mirror, he stuck out his chest and laughed. Then, he walked away and didn't see my dirty look.

After dinner, when I literally wrote out what he said to me, I had the perfect comeback: Maybe I won't ever grow out—like your brain. In the moment though, my tongue was twisted, and my brain was mush, so I didn't say anything. Just like when I'm at school. It's weird how that happens, even with my brother.

Nate wasn't dumb. I was words, he was numbers. He was very good at math, but when it came to reading and writing, he couldn't seem to get it together. However, with a little help from me, his words were just fine. He said my written words were better, but I was starting to leave more and more room for him to fill in the blanks on his assignments. I loved my brother and would do anything for him, even though he was a jerk sometimes.

My best writing happens when I'm propped up on my bed surrounded by pillows and stuffed animals. A purple bear from Build-A-Bear Workshop that I named Lily is my favorite. So, it was sitting like this that I decided to write to Betty again.

Dear Betty,

Hello and how are you doing? I hope you received my letter last week.

My parents just had a family meeting and announced that we are moving to Chicago! How am I going to start over somewhere else? Did it take a long time to get used to living in your new home? It must have been difficult, especially without your husband.

Why am I so afraid to talk to people? Even if I do something good, it's hard to be proud of myself. Does anyone else notice? Does anyone care? If anyone ever says that I have done a good job, I always think I could have done better.

Will I ever be enough just the way I am?

Your pen pal,

Grace Elizabeth

6. Goodbye Connie, Hello Chicago

I thought saying goodbye to Connie would be difficult. I didn't know it would be one of the worst days in my life.

Connie was in my class from the beginning at Stanton Elementary School, but I didn't think we would ever be friends. We were both somewhat plain Jane, but not really unattractive either. She was tall, like me, but "big boned," as my mother would say. Her hair was light, maybe even a strawberry blonde, and fell straight down her back. Sometimes she wore it in a braid, and oh, how I envied her on those days!

The funny thing about my hair is that it doesn't even grow down, just out. Braiding it is a nightmare. If I want to do something different but easy, I wear a headband, which makes my brain itch after a while. Mostly I use a hair tie to control the awfulness.

Connie had a loud laugh, partly because her mouth opened extra wide. Her brown eyes always laughed with her. My laughs came in ripples, so it was a good combination. Connie called my eyes brown too, but they're hazel like my dad's.

Because she laughed louder than anyone in second grade, at first I thought she was obnoxious. As I got to know her, I looked forward to hearing that laugh. Is there any sound in the world sweeter than a friend laughing? Well, maybe the sound of two friends laughing together is just as nice.

We started to become friends at the religious classes our parents made us go to. On Sundays after Mass, we were dropped off for Catholic lessons specifically for kids who didn't go to Catholic school. Connie and I called them our Jesus lessons, then later just Jeez.

There is a lot to learn to be a good Catholic. You have no idea. The real uniform-wearing Catholics have a bit of a leg up I suppose. We had to make do with just Jeez knowledge. I didn't complain, mind you, I only had to go on Sundays. Those poor kids had Jesus lessons every school day.

We both got phones in fifth and texted each other enough that our parents lectured us about screen time. It's always been difficult for me to make friends. The girls I did hang around with at school would often leave me out of games they were playing. But with Connie, I knew I had someone.

At recess one day, I told her she was my best friend. Connie My Constant, I called her. To have a best friend is magic. It's important that at least one person in this world thinks you are funny, prettier than plain, and somewhat normal. A best friend can do that, and I had one.

On a typical Jeez Sunday, Dad was a stickler for getting me to class on time. Sister Catherine David was in charge. "You two in the back, hush!" said Sister. Seems like we were constantly marching in and out of church for one thing or another, always in height order. Sister Catherine wasn't exactly mean, but she was no Sister Act fun nun. Connie and I were the two tallest girls, last in line, and we found it hilarious.

When we received First Communion in second grade, our folded hands held little white prayer books as we paraded in tiny slow steps up the center aisle of church. Connie whispered to me, "We are brides of Christ." Where did she even hear that? It didn't matter. We still lost it in a fit of giggles.

I was proud of the little notebook where I kept a record of all the sacraments I had received. Baptism,

Confession, Communion ... check, check, check. Confirmation would happen next. When I realized that one of the sacraments was an actual death prep, I stopped keeping track. C'mon, Extreme Unction, gimme a break.

Our last Jeez class before summer break was just two weeks after my parents told us we were moving. I didn't know when I would see Connie again and wanted to say goodbye. We ended class with the Our Father prayer as usual. I went into the hallway to wait for her as she stuffed her missal and song sheets into her backpack. Standing there, I took out my phone and scrolled to the latest Instagram story she'd posted and couldn't believe what I was seeing. It was a boomerang video of Connie opening her bedroom door and saying, "G-bye dork," then closing it. Opening, closing, opening, closing, g-bye dork, g-bye dork, g-bye dork. Was this supposed to be funny?

She filmed herself at the door of her very pink bedroom, with a teeny tiny cartoon image of a girl with curly hair and glasses pasted on the doorknob in the video. Was that supposed to be me?

Connie rushed out of the classroom. My mouth was dry and probably hanging open. I held up the phone. For a second, no words would come out.

Then I was sputtering, "I guess you made this with help from the girls that we both said we didn't like."

"Oh, I know. I'm sorry. They made me do it."

"How did they make you do it?"

"They said that I wouldn't be able to sit with them at lunch if I didn't do it."

"Were you just pretending to be my friend?"

"No, I like you … but it's hard to describe."

"Try me." I could feel my face getting red.

Connie hesitated, and then blurted it all out. "You can be super serious sometimes. I know we laugh together, but it's because I'm the one who is funny. You hardly ever even say anything, and it's just not fun to be around you anymore. We're becoming so different."

This was news to me. I had lots of texts that said we were friends.

Connie didn't wait for me to respond. "You love to read and you're always writing in that little notebook. Or sending letters to those old people you don't even know. It's because you don't like to talk. I think it's kinda good timing that you're moving."

My "best friend" was glad I was taking my loser self to Chicago. Good to know.

I turned and left her standing there without saying anything else. I wanted to walk away before

I started to cry. Mom said something to me as I got into the car, but it was drowned out by the sniveling in my head. The drive home seemed to take forever and as much as I wanted a hug from my mom, I couldn't tell her what had happened. She has lots of friends and now once again I was an underachiever.

My bed felt like the warm cuddle I needed. It was time to write something and make the failure feelings go away.

Edith lived in Mobile, Alabama and I thought from her profile that she'd be the best person to answer my questions about people.

Dear Edith,

Hello and how are you? I can see online that one of your favorite activities is reading mystery novels. Do they keep you guessing, or do you figure out the murderer before the end of the story? I bet you are very good at picking up the clues.

How do I get better at that in real life?

Not to guess a murderer, of course, but how do I truly know who my friends are? It's been a question mark so far.

What are the clues? Did you ever think that someone was your friend but then it turned out that it wasn't true?

My friend who I will call "C" was nice and we did lots of silly things together. Now I am going to move far away, and she made fun of me on social media for all the world to see. She's honestly glad that I am moving away!

I should probably read mystery stories, too. Maybe it will help me solve the biggest question of my life right now. Why don't I have any "come over to my house and hang out" friends? I hope you are enjoying all your activities and friends! Please know that I am thinking about you.

Thank you for reading.

Your pen pal friend,

Grace Elizabeth

7. Moving

For the next month, the Mackenzie frenzy took over. Mom had a million things for us to do in preparation for the move. And by "us," I mean me. Nate did not lift a finger while I helped Mom sort and haul plastic baby toys, old clothes, and junk to thrift stores.

As we got in the car for our third trip to town that day, Mom tried to be nonchalant, but I knew it was killing her. "So, you haven't spent much time with Connie lately."

"No, she was for real glad that we're moving."

"Oh my. What did she say?"

"That we've outgrown each other." Even though I detested air quotes and anyone who used them, I made them with an exaggerated "ewww" face. It made me feel like I was getting back at Connie for that mean and stupid video. Mom's reaction told me I was right.

"Honey, I am so sorry."

"Nothing to be sorry about. Maybe she was right." I smiled even though it still hurt. Mom replied with a pity grin and when we came back to the house, I ran right up to my room.

Dad missed some of the drama because he was traveling back and forth to Chicago to prepare for the move. He was home now and busy in his "office" before taking one last trip. Really, he just had a desk in the corner of our basement, which had a musty smell and all sorts of creepy crawly things on the walls. I could hear him walk up the two flights of stairs to talk to Mom.

The whispering from their bedroom was easily drowned out by my earbuds. Mom was obviously bringing him up to speed while she helped him pack. Then, his heavy suitcase thumped down the stairs followed by more steps coming back. I hate it when my parents feel sorry for me.

"Grace?" Dad poked his head in my room.

I lifted my blankets.

"Mom told me what happened, and I just wanted to check to see if you were okay before I head out."

"Yeah, I'm okay. At least I know how she feels about me."

"Well, know that friendships can come and go, but you will always have your mom and me. We believe in you, and I know you will find some great friends after you're settled in your new school."

"Thanks, Dad." I tried my best smile, which included teeth. I even tried to make my eyes smile. I don't think he bought it though. Dad was pretty good at reading people. I thought I was good at reading people too. But after Connie, apparently not.

Dad kissed me on the top of my head and left my room without saying anything else. He had been searching for his A-list job and now he had it. I wanted him to be happy, but the truth was that I never thought my dad was cool enough to write TV commercials. Some of the other men at the ad agency wore jeans and didn't even shave. The women certainly didn't dress like Mom. Their jeans were ripped and kind of tight. Dad, clean-shaven and in his khaki pants, somehow always looked a bit geeky to me.

I wondered if he would make work friends in Chicago.

8. Our New House

Dad arranged for a moving company to pack up our whole house before we left. It wasn't the first time I flew on a plane, but it was still fun. When we got to Chicago, another company came and unpacked everything. I arranged my room exactly as it was before and had even picked the same color blue for the walls. Honestly, so much was changing, I couldn't cope with four new walls.

It was our new address that did me in. Our parents bought a house at 247 Gone Away Court. Can you believe it? It's not enough that we had to leave everything we knew behind, but every day, our address was a 24/7 reminder that we had "gone away." It sounded weirdly strange, and I looked at the street sign for many days in a row expecting it to be a joke. It wasn't.

Our new house was bigger. There was an extra bedroom which was now Dad's actual office. Mom ordered bookshelves and a small filing cabinet plus a big calendar for his desk. She fussed with the knickknacks on the desk and what to put up on the wall. At the end of the day, Mom would probably be using the office herself anyway.

"Do you think he will like it?" She twisted her head, looking at the little cup of pens. Who cares? is what I wanted to say. But she seemed so intent on making every detail perfect.

When Dad finally saw his new office setup, he looked quickly and said, "Nice." I could tell Mom was disappointed.

9. New But Thinking of Old

Getting to Chicago was easy, but it did not feel like home. I wondered when that would happen.

First, we were not in the city of Chicago. We lived in Oak View, which is right outside Chicago. After seeing the high school where Nate would go, we drove past my school. They were just a few blocks apart.

The building itself was major, stretching for a huge block. The windows were decorated with kids' art projects, like my old school only with lots more construction paper taped to the glass. I was nervous about finding my way around. Mom arranged for a tour after we were settled. The halls were wide and went forever with gray shiny lockers as far as I could see. There was a science room, an art room, and a huge theater where the band also practiced.

Mom was duly impressed. She looked extremely happy, there was no way I could be a stick in the mud.

"Oh, would you look at that, Gracie, a beautiful stage and actual theater seats!"

And why shouldn't she be happy? She's going to work in the school library Monday, Wednesday, and Friday. In fact, there was already a black plaque at the checkout counter: Lisa Anne Mackenzie, Asst. Librarian.

I wasn't too upset that she would be at my school. Honestly, it could have been worse—a teacher. That would have been too embarrassing for words as the new kid.

Nate made friends immediately at his school. He had started to run and train with some of the football team boys right away and worked that "bro" connection. After practice, they all hung out at a different house every day. One guy from the team named Mike started to come to our house and tagged along everywhere with Nate. They ate popcorn and played video games. The family room smelled like rotten cheese, which was probably from their farts that I could hear from the kitchen. I never went near them. Nate was glad to avoid me too.

Our new neighborhood was a cute town with a Mister Softee ice cream truck that drove up and down our streets in the afternoon. It must be a small-town thing. Once I heard that tune, I couldn't get it out of my head. Everything seemed right with the world with a creamsicle in one hand and a book in the other.

Still, it felt strange to be separated from family. Before we moved, Grammy loved to visit on Sundays and always had something to say about Mom being excessively skinny or working too much. Her name was Olivia Marie, but everyone called her Ollie. She never liked that nickname.

As our only grandparent, Grammy was not like other kids' grandmothers who always made cookies for them. Instead, she loved to talk about her adventures and having fun with friends on trips to the casinos in Atlantic City (Do they have casinos in Chicago?). Also, Grammy is not the letter writing type. She told me that once. Although now that I'm far away, maybe she'll reconsider.

Still, I needed to write to someone, and Florence popped up. Florence has lived in Maine her whole life. She likes to garden and sounds pretty different from Grammy.

Dear Florence,

I don't know much about where you live, but I am picturing a very cozy place where everyone knows everyone else. Is that true? Do you have many friends from your childhood that you are still friends with now?

I also think Maine is very cold from what I see on the weather map. Your garden must have plants that like those temperatures. What are your favorite flowers? My mom does not have much of a green thumb and most of her plants die within a few months. The bright side of that was we didn't have to move any plants to our new house in Chicago.

There are people who are thinking of you. I hope you get outside to garden in the spring.

Your pen pal friend,

Grace Elizabeth

PS: I have an Aunt Florence, but everyone calls her Flossy. Is that your nickname?

10. A New School

The start of the school year was the official reminder that my friend counter started at zero. On Monday, Wednesday and Friday, Mom would take me to school. On the other days I would take the bus, which stopped at the corner of our street. Mom had already met my teacher, Ms. Infante, and said that I would like her.

Besides searching for pen pal Florence, I spent the past few nights searching online for "how to fit in" hints at my new school. Join clubs—check. Find a mentor—what? How do I do that? Trust me, I had to laugh when I read about "initiating a conversation." It took me about two years to talk to Connie. How do people even do that? Google is not that helpful for a middle school kid.

On the first day my stomach was churning. It felt nice to have Mom there, but it was her first day of school too, so I could tell she was nervous. Those nails were looking terrible once again. Mom saw Ms.

Infante down the hall and gave me a head nod in that direction. And then she was off.

"Hello Grace, come on in." Ms. Infante smiled. "Welcome to seventh grade." Everyone stopped and stared when I was introduced as the 'new girl' to the Chicago area. I wanted to blend in, but that was hard to do because I had clearly missed the call about what to wear.

I noticed immediately that most of the girls wore bras. Mom had given me the option at one point in the summer, but I couldn't adjust the straps correctly and they dug into me. So, I stuck with my cotton undershirt. Black and navy blue seemed to be the go-to colors for outerwear even though blue and white were the school colors. Everyone was staring at my shoes and smiling ... not the nice kind of smiles.

I really like colors. My sneakers were pink, which complemented my purple and blue T-shirt and jeans. Some of the girls had extra stuff on their jeans like embroidery and buttons, and one even had lace. I had none of the above.

Because Nate had a heads-up from the football dudes, he was already wearing an appropriate T-shirt. There was no team to give me a wardrobe alert.

Grace's Write Time

I got out my pen and a notebook right away and started writing things down like I knew what I was doing. It was a list of certifiable wrongs: hair, nails, jacket, underwear. Super concentration was the name of the game as I looked like I was writing the Declaration of Independence. Everyone was staring at me but quickly got bored and went back to being seventh graders.

With the no phones during class time rule, distraction strategies are important. Fortunately, they are second nature to a nerd like me.

11. A Letter

That first day was a half day and the mail was already delivered by the time I got home. In it was a letter from Connie. I hadn't heard from her all summer—out of sight, out of mind apparently. I texted her a few pics of our new house, but she never responded. I must've been desperate to keep the connection. Our moms were somewhat friendly, which must have been where she got our address.

> *Dear Grace,*
>
> *It's not the same without you. I am sorry for making that stupid video. Just found out that I'm in Mrs. Smith's class—you know, the teacher who always yelled at us when we came back into school after recess.*
>
> *Our family still goes to church. But in my last year of Jeez classes, there is nothing to look forward to every Sunday.*

> *I have to go, but wanted to let you know that I was thinking about you. I know how much you like writing and wanted to write this personal letter. Let me know if you like your new house.*
>
> *Your address is crazy! Gone Away Court? I told some of the other girls and we laughed—but a nice laugh.*
>
> *Love,*
>
> *Connie Your Constant*

She seemed sorry and I didn't know what to think. Maybe I would text her later. When a friend says she's sorry, what do you do? Christ forgave his enemies, and I could give it a try, but wasn't in the mood at that moment.

One good thing about moving, though—no more Jeez classes. However, I did meet my one and only best friend at Jeez school, even if she did betray me.

After my mom gave me Connie's letter, she started making my favorite peanut butter fluff sandwiches, telling me about all the things she was doing at school.

"Things are quite a bit different in Illinois. The state requirements are rigorous and there are different programs available for all kinds of students who are gifted or challenged in some way."

I started to zone out, but Connie's letter somehow gave me the courage to ask my mom for the one thing that bothered me about school. I interrupted her.

"Mom, do you think I need a bra?"

"Oh, do you want one now?" She stopped fussing with lunch and turned to look right at my chest.

"Maybe. Most of the girls are wearing them and I'm just not sure."

"Well, that's good timing for this weekend. We can go and try some in town and then order them online if we find a brand that you like."

I went upstairs to my room and stared at myself in my undershirt. What if I don't like wearing a bra? I turned in front of the mirror. Should I write back to Connie? I turned back. Am I a total dork?

Whether or not I wrote back to her would have to wait. I had more important things to think about … like my underwear.

12. New School New Friends

At my new school the hallway was endlessly long. The people at the end of it looked like dolls. For each class, we had to change rooms. I don't mean to say that my old school was like a one-room schoolhouse from Little House on the Prairie, but almost.

Because the first day had been a blessed half day, it was impossible to get too nervous when I could go home at noon and eat lunch in our kitchen. It was the second day that was giving me the sweats. As lunchtime approached, I almost ran. In the cafeteria, I only saw eyeballs. Why did I wear this ugly purple sweater? But just as soon as I sat down, three other girls joined me.

"Hey, are you Grace Mackenzie? Any relation to Nate Mackenzie on the football team?"

"Yeah, he's my brother."

"Nice to meet you. I'm Patty and this is Becky and Janet. Did you just move here?"

"Yes, from Pennsylvania."

They put their trays down on the table. Patty and Becky were eating grilled cheese sandwiches and French fries. Janet had red Jell-O and an apple.

Becky took over as the talkative one, "Patty has an older sister at the high school. We saw your brother's picture on the football program. He played on the varsity at his old school, so that must mean he's pretty good."

"Yeah, I guess so." The last thing I wanted to talk about was Nate.

"Are you going to the game on Friday?"

"Yeah, I'll probably go with my parents."

"We'll be there if you want to sit with us."

It was nice having someone to eat lunch with. Patty and Becky were in my grade, but not in Ms. Infante's homeroom. Janet was in my homeroom. Once I wrote their names down, I laughed out loud. Their initials spelled PB&J—my second favorite sandwich. The peanut butter must be crunchy though. What's the point of eating anything unless you can crunch it?

We ate lunch together the rest of the week. Patty and Becky had matching brown ponytails that they liked to throw over their shoulders when they laughed. They both wore trendy clothes, but not too girly or frilly. Maybe they have older sisters.

Janet liked to wear her blonde hair down. They talked a lot to each other about stuff I knew nothing about as I tried to get caught up on their favorite topics. Football Friday was getting closer and, I had to admit, I was starting to get excited about my new school.

13. Mr. J

My favorite classes were new ones like chorus, art, and social studies—things I didn't do at my old school. But the class that I looked forward to the most was writing, officially called Language Arts. We were going to learn how to write essays and stories and the course outline listed a story writing contest at the end of the year. I had never entered a writing contest before.

Mr. Janowski said that we should call him Mr. J and he looked like the bookworm type. His glasses were seriously thick, and his clothes were on the nerdy side. Every day he wore the same thing: khaki pants and a blue shirt. I wanted to give him the benefit of the doubt that it was not the same blue shirt and khaki pants, but time would tell.

He was pumped to show us around the classroom. Once we were in our seats, he pointed above the blackboard that wasn't used anymore and said, "We will be talking about the difference between essays and stories. The elements of a good essay are all here for you!" He had taped posters up high that explained the foundation of writing stories and essays. I was pretty much in the know already because I was used to helping Nate with similar assignments.

We began to discuss the basic parts of a story, like setting. Where is the story taking place? Is it the current day or in the past or future? Who are the characters? Mr. J gave us our own copy of a writing handout called Story Mountain that we would work on together.

He went on to explain, "After the setting and characters are determined, what is the 'rising action' of the story?" Mr. J promised we would discuss each one of these things in detail.

He stopped to tuck in his shirt. He waved his arms around a lot and his shirt hung out in the back. Mr. J continued, "Next is the 'story summit.' What is the problem? What went wrong that needs to be fixed? That will lead into the 'falling action.'"

When I'm bored, I sometimes make up stories in my head. In church or at a store, I look around and wonder ... how did these people get here? What is their issue to be solved? What is the lesson learned? How are they different at the end of the story? That little nugget is the best part.

An essay, Mr. Janowski pointed out, is typically a personal statement about a specific topic. A story can be totally made up. We were going to practice both. The end of a story must not be stupidly obvious. That's boring. Duh. But it got me thinking about my own story. Did I have anything interesting to say? How will my friendship story end?

14. Nate

It didn't take long for Nate to start asking me for help with his Language Arts projects. He could do the math easy peasy, but just hated any type of writing assignment. He always waited until the last minute to ask for help and that drove me nuts.

"Grace, how long do you think it will take you to write this essay for me? It's due tomorrow." The topic 'What was the most unexpected or difficult part of your first day of school?' was easy for me because we both had real first days.

Thanks to Mr. J, I was able to provide just the right guidance. I plopped down on his bed, opened my laptop, and started coaching. Nate probably thought I would just write the whole thing for him. What was the fun in that?

"Nate, it's super important that you start your essay with a good hook to get your reader's attention. Then you need to build your paragraphs with a main idea and supporting evidence. If you have more than one idea or a few paragraphs, you should write a transition statement in between each to separate them. Finally, end with your conclusion, summarizing your main points."

"You mean you're not going to write this out for me?"

"I have my own homework, but I will proofread it for you."

"Oh Grace, c'mon. I can't write like you!"

Honestly, it felt good to be needed, but he had so many things going right for him. If we were really keeping score, he was killing it in the friend zone. They were at our house a lot, sprawling all over the sofa, hogging the entire family room. Not that I would ever sit with them.

Nate and his friends were obsessed with social media and on their phones almost all the time. He wasn't always like that. But now, most days he was absorbed in a Snapstreak. Why isn't one Snapchat ever enough? He had to keep the streak going. That's why he never had time for his homework.

Yes, they were all obnoxious. But they seemed to already have formed a loyal connection. Or maybe it was the constant supply of snacks Mom kept in the pantry that his friends ate nonstop.

I didn't feel bad that Nate had to actually work at something. I snapped my computer shut and left him speechless.

15. Social Media

Honestly, I think social media has just made being a kid harder. All the teenagers I know have their noses in a phone constantly.

I think I get it. As an almost teenager, I wondered: did Connie feel pressure to put me on her reject list? I didn't have a phone until fifth grade. Then, social media was where I went if I got bored. But it didn't rule my life. It's important to pay attention to the people I am with and not look at videos of other goofy stuff.

But honestly, sometimes it's easier to just get lost in stories and reels, especially about people who are more interesting than I am. Will anyone ever want to start a Snapstreak with me?

16. Friday Night Football

Friday night football finally came. It was Nate's first game and Mom and Dad wanted to sit with me, but I had made other plans. It felt strange to be there with someone else and not rely on my parents. I think they were as surprised as I was.

Everyone was talking about the game at school that day, which would be at the high school home field. After meeting PB&J at the snack bar, we found our way to the student section and sat a few rows up from the field. I could see Mom and Dad in the parent section. Nate would probably be sitting on the bench, but we wanted to be supportive. I could tell he was nervous because even up in the stands, I could hear him talking very loudly.

At halftime, Nate still had not played in the game. I went to get hot chocolate, and Janet said she wanted to tag along. Her hair was in a ponytail and she twirled it in between taking sips and scooping mini marshmallows out of her drink.

"Do you think your brother will play at all?" asked Janet.

"I don't know—he's new on the team."

As soon as the third quarter started, I had to go back to the snack bar because the bathroom was there. Maybe that large hot chocolate was not such a great idea. Janet saved our seats, since for some reason Patty and Becky had not come back to the stands.

I was in one of the stalls at the end of the row when the bathroom door opened to high-pitched giggling. It was Patty's laugh for sure, and I was just about to call out when I heard Becky's voice.

"She is a bit odd, don't you think?"

"What did you think of her clothes? Does her mom shop for her?"

"Well, they're from Hicksville, what'd ya expect?"

"Yeah, but Nate is hot. I don't care where he's from."

"I think he saw us when we were close to the field!"

"Do you think we can be nice enough to her for the next couple weeks so that we're invited to their house?"

Not again.

I flushed. Dead silence followed. When I opened the door and came face-to-face with the two nasties, I couldn't think of anything to say, as usual. They watched me leave without a word. The crowd was screaming, and I was careful not to trip on the bleachers climbing up to where Mom and Dad were sitting. It was then I realized that I had forgotten to wash my hands.

"Mom, do you have any hand sanitizer?"

The gel had a nice lavender scent, and I rubbed and rubbed to wipe away all traces of PB&J.

17. Letters to the Rescue

Nate was shoveling the last of the Lucky Charms into his mouth as fast as he could the next morning. It looked like Mom was about to get on his case but changed her mind. I had no energy to argue, and I slammed the pantry door looking for the Rice Krispies.

"Are you okay?" Mom asked.

"Yes, just a little tired after the game," I sighed.

"Yeah, you worked uber-hard last night." Nate laughed. I could barely understand him with his mouth full, milk dripping out in between bites.

Because Nate was technically still a JV player, the coach only subbed him in if they were winning by a large margin. He was put into the game toward the end of the fourth quarter along with the backup quarterback. It didn't matter to Nate, and he caught a terrific pass for many yards (I told you I was not great at math, so no, I don't know the exact number).

Nate was pleased with himself and honestly deserved the Lucky Charms that morning. The win was assured way before the end of the game, but still, everyone was mightily impressed with his catch and congratulated us as we were leaving.

After breakfast, Mom and Dad seemed eager to move on to something else and left the house as I loaded the dishwasher. It was pretty good timing for me as I had a lot to say and went right up to my room. I wasn't planning on talking to anyone, mind you.

In honor of our new address, I selected a senior named Mildred from Chicago that I found on the Sunrise Seniors website. I am not sure exactly where she was living in Chicago. Sunrise kept that a secret but having her close by felt nice … and it seemed like Mildred could use a distraction.

Mildred recently fell and broke her hip, so she spent her days watching westerns on TV with her cat, Doodles. She used to love to go to the movies with her friends but didn't see them much now due to being sidelined with her hip. That had to be extra awful.

Dear Mildred,

Hello and how are you doing? I read about your hip, and I am sorry that you are not able to move around. How do you feed Doodles? How did your cat get its name?

I have a question for you because I am new to the Chicago area and am looking to make friends. Is there a secret to friendship? It's hard for me to get to know people and they seem to like me at first, but then don't stick around for very long.

My new school is big, and I am doing things for the first time ever like chorus and writing class. Our writing teacher is having a contest at the end of the year. I will send you what I write.

I am trying to be more social and do things with other people, but it's been hard moving to a new city and starting at a large school.

Your notice in Sunrise Seniors also said that you love western movies. I used to go to the movies with my Grammy when we lived in Pennsylvania, but now there is no one to go with.

Do you have a favorite western movie? Mine is True Grit. Now that's something I need more of!

My mom says that families with both parents working full time should not have pets. So, hug your kitty cat for me. I will be thinking of you.

Hugs,

Your pen pal,

Grace Elizabeth

18. Back at School Back at Home

It felt good to ignore PB&J on Monday morning, but that feeling quickly disappeared when the lunch bell rang. I was dreading lunch and almost didn't go, but *A Wrinkle in Time* was in my backpack.

The bell rang soon enough, and we were back in class. Thank goodness it was writing with Mr. J, who said he would be assigning more essays before we started to write stories. Mr. J wanted to get an idea of our writing skill level, so the essay about our first day of school was just the beginning. Today's lesson was about choosing our own essay topic. Mr. J would be suggesting topics, but we could also be creative. "Write what you know," he said as he walked up and down the aisles. My dream was to travel and write about faraway places, but for that moment, I took Mr. J's advice.

I still had not decided on any of my essay details. We were supposed to list at least five possible topics.

When I got home, Mom was in the kitchen getting dinner ready while I poured some apple juice.

"Everything okay? You didn't say much over the weekend about your friends from the football game."

I couldn't decide if I should chug my juice and get up to my bed nest of covers, books, and Spotify, or tell my mom the real story about PB&J. I decided to split it down the middle.

"Well, yeah, about that—it wasn't much fun. Turns out they were looking to meet Nate somehow. Obviously, he's the only Mackenzie kid worth knowing."

"Oh honey, you know that is not true. If they said that, they're mean, and you don't want to be friends with them."

It was a good thing I decided not to tell Mom every detail from Friday night. I didn't want to distract her from making Nate's favorite spaghetti and meatball dinner. As she pulled out all the ingredients from the cabinets, Mom followed up with one of the most dreaded sentences heard by kids all over the world.

"You know what you need?" she said, closing the fridge with a thud.

Oh no—what will this pronouncement be? Tea and toast? Junk food? A day at the museum? Not that I would mind that at all. Maybe I could go by myself.

"Some exercise!"

Oh joy. There it was.

Mom continued, "You know Nate made friends very quickly with the guys from the football team. It's all about camaraderie. Doing things together—that's the basis of friendship for kids today. Frankly, it's the basis of friendship for just about any age." She started to open cans of crushed tomatoes in earnest. "If you want friends, you know what I always say: teamwork makes the dream work."

I wasn't sure that saying was all about friendships, but I got the point. It was only a matter of time before we were back to sports talk. In Pennsylvania pioneer style, Mom started the lady's softball league back home. By the time we moved, it was up to eight teams.

Every spring, there was a mother-daughter game. I only played once and I can say without hesitation that it was the worst day of my life—until I lost my best friend, that is. I struck out every time, except for the time that I hit a ball by accident. It dribbled only a few feet in front of me and I ran like crazy for first base. I was almost there but then fell face-first in the dirt and was tagged out.

Mom said not to worry about it and that we had "plenty of time" for lessons in the future. I never reminded her of when that plenty of time would kick in for real. She did take me to a batting cage once. I hit the first ball and it almost whacked her in the head. It was not pretty. We decided to leave at that point. At least I was "batting a thousand."

Dad played Division III football in college at one of the million Pennsylvania universities that take sports way too seriously. Nate's apple fell directly from both of those trees. My apple was apparently rotten to the core.

Over the years, Mom always tried to be encouraging. Naming me Grace was her Hail Mary prayer for the coordination that she hoped one day would magically appear. It looked like I dodged a bullet with the move to Illinois. Mom was distracted with her new school, and we would not be fielding grounders any time soon. Really though, I was never quite sure anyone in the world had ever dodged a bullet. Especially not me.

19. Exercise Is Good for Me

The fastest way to end any discussion with Mom was to do what she asked. I might not have been great with a baseball bat, but I could go for a walk without hurting anyone. What harm could come from a bit of fresh air in my lungs?

Our street is a dead-end cul-de-sac, so I went up to the main road and took a right. The sidewalk stretched ahead of me for about a mile but then faded out. Long legs and a rotten sense of direction is not a great combination. With only one turn, how lost could I get?

After a while the sidewalk ended, and from the grassy dirt edge of the road, a black gate opened to a long gravel driveway. A sign on the post read "Hawthorne Stables."

I didn't know much about horses, but what the heck? Time to investigate. Off the driveway, I started down a long wood chip path that led to a red and white barn which was next to a gorgeous house and a couple of sheds.

Behind the barn was a huge dirt arena with a white fence surrounding it. A woman dressed in cool looking pants stood in the middle of the fenced area, giving orders to six riders. All the horses were walking around a track. I couldn't hear what she said, but suddenly they were trotting around the ring with the riders jumping up and down in their saddles. I started to laugh, but the riders were deadly serious, so I stifled it. Looking at all that bouncing, I clutched my chest and remembered that Mom and I were going to order bras. Looks like that would be a necessary item for any woman on a horse.

At first, I thought the riders were adults. But when I got closer, I could see that they were kids about my age. Everyone was dressed nicely with a jacket, helmet, snug pants, and boots. One of the boys was in my homeroom. I knew him!

His name was Andrew Cassidy and Ms. Infante had asked us both to get supplies from the stationery closet in the room down the hall last week. "Call me Andy," he had said. His dark brown, almost black curly hair was kind of wild. He had a face full of freckles and blue eyes. Of course, now I couldn't see the curly hair because of his helmet, but I knew it was him.

Andy had insisted on carrying the paper and pens back to the classroom, but he was all legs and arms, and almost tripped over his own feet. Anyway, Call Me Andy was now riding expertly. I guess he's better at sitting in a saddle than walking in a hallway.

The woman at the center of the ring had a long stick with a little rope at the end of it and looked like she was conducting an orchestra. The trotting and bouncing went on for a while as she reminded the riders, "Balance is the key. Remember to keep your weight evenly distributed in your saddle. Nice work Jackie. Eyes up, heels down. Shoulders back."

She walked around the center of the ring and shouted, "Great posture, Andy! Keep up the good work. Strive for an even tempo. Try to be one with your horse as you move. This is what makes a comfortable ride. You are speaking to your horse with your touch. Now, change."

With that, the horses started galloping around the ring. I was standing on the bottom rung of the fence to get the best view. It looked like bouncy fun as Andy rode past me.

The lesson was ending, and Andy waved to me. I decided to follow him to the barn. It was getting late, and I still had to walk home. The instructor came up to me.

"Hi, I'm Chris. Have you ever ridden before?"

"No, I haven't been around horses at all."

"Well, our horses are all very friendly, so we'd love to have you if you want to give it a try."

I smiled, but wanted to ask Andy questions that Chris couldn't hear.

He was busy taking off his saddle and hanging up the reins.

"Hi Grace." I was surprised he remembered my name.

"Hey, Andy. How long have you been taking lessons?"

"It's kind of new." Then in a low voice he said, "I can tell you more about it later at school."

Why was he whispering? I tiptoed a bit closer to Andy and his horse.

"His name is Clyde. I always ride him when I'm here."

Clyde had a smooth and shiny coat that glistened red in the arena. In the barn, he looked brown and quite huge up close, but I could also see that he was gentle, patiently waiting for Andy to hang up the saddle. I reached out to put my hand on Clyde's neck and felt him breathing. Suddenly Clyde turned to look at me with the biggest brown eyes I'd ever seen. I stepped away, frightened at first. But Clyde didn't move another muscle.

"I think he likes you," Andy said. "Want to stay and help me brush?"

"No, that's okay. I need to go. It's probably time for dinner at home." My heart started to beat faster. Everything was new and the barn smelled like horse poop, which I guess was normal.

"Okay, see you later."

Chris yelled over to me as I headed back down the path. "You are welcome back anytime."

I ran most of the way home but couldn't stop thinking about Clyde and, of course, Andy.

20. Andy

The next day Mom gave me a ride to school. I was debating whether to talk to her about riding lessons when I saw Andy waiting in front of the school psychologist's office at the end of the hallway. As soon as he saw me, he made a beeline for the stairs.

When the lunch bell rang, he waited for me at our homeroom door, and we walked to the cafeteria together. I wondered if he was a new kid too; it didn't look like he was planning on sitting with anyone.

At lunch, I was even more curious about what was going on.

"Why did you leave in such a hurry this morning?"

"I was waiting for Mrs. Z, the school psychologist."

"Yeah, what for? Oh, never mind, I guess that's none of my business. Don't worry, I don't need to know."

"No, I want to tell you. You're, like … safe. Being new and all."

I couldn't help but laugh at what certainly did not sound like a compliment.

Andy fumbled, "I didn't mean …"

"No worries," I jumped in. I knew Andy wasn't trying to hurt my feelings.

"It's just that you're new and you don't know many people yet, so you won't be blabbing about me all over the school."

"True," I said, still not sure where this was going.

"Okay. Well, you know how I'm taking those riding lessons?" I nodded. "They're part of a counseling program I'm doing called equine therapy."

"Equi-what?"

"It's called 'equine therapy,' and it's for people that have issues."

"What kind of issues?"

Andy looked around and lowered his voice.

"I have trouble concentrating on stuff. I can get started on one thing, get distracted, start something else, never finish the first thing. It's all a big cycle that can start all over again."

I was nodding. "Well, that happens to me too."

Andy lowered his voice again. "I don't tell everyone this, but I'm adopted. My parents love me, and I know that, but sometimes, I also get angry and just think I can't do anything right."

"Is it because you are adopted?"

"No—I mean—yes. Well, I'm not exactly sure. I have a lot of questions."

"But how does equine therapy help you?"

"It's all about the horses. You were close to Clyde for a few minutes. Did you feel it? When I am taking care of Clyde—petting, brushing, washing—it's an amazing feeling. Sometimes I'm just nervous for no reason. After my lesson, I get to work with another person to take care of Clyde, and am responsible for his grooming and feeding. I can't explain it, but when I am with Clyde, my mind is quiet and calm. Some days when I don't have a lesson, I like to walk him around the property."

"You just walk him?"

Andy smiled and I could almost read his thoughts: I bet this girl thinks I'm nuts. But then he continued, "Yes, but I talk to him too. He's a good listener." Andy bit into his apple, which was a good time for me to ask more questions.

"Is everyone in your riding class also doing equine therapy?"

"I'm the only one. You saw me during a regular riding lesson. My counselor is usually with me on another day and we walk, talk, and sometimes ride together. I'm on Clyde, and Chris gives my therapist another horse."

Mom had made a peanut butter and jelly sandwich for lunch. When the bell rang, I looked down, and it was gone. I ate it super fast but forgot to eat my chips

Andy leaned in a bit and pleaded. "Please don't tell anyone about me being adopted or the equine therapy."

"Oh, no. I won't say anything. I thought the horses were beautiful and was thinking of asking my mom if I could take lessons."

"That would be fantastic! See if your parents can talk to Chris about joining my class. We are starting a new Saturday riding group, and it would be fun if you could take your lessons with me."

We walked back to homeroom together, and I felt happy that I was keeping a secret. It wasn't that I needed to know the details of Andy's backstory, but he trusted me enough to tell me something very personal. Isn't that what a friend does?

21. Horseback Riding Lessons

Mom was busy in the kitchen when I walked in. "Grace, would you please set the table for dinner? Nate will be home late from practice today and I would like everything ready."

"Sure."

I wanted the horseback riding conversation to be no big deal, but knew I would be crushed if Mom said no.

"Mom, you must hear stuff in the library about the kids at school. Did I tell you that there is a guy named Andy in my class? And guess what, today he told me that he's adopted. Did you know that?"

I know I promised Andy I wouldn't tell anyone, but my mom didn't count, did she? Besides, she needed to know the real story if I wanted to take lessons.

"Grace, I have taught you better. You know perfectly well that I am not going to say anything about the students I meet at the library."

"Did you know he's adopted?"

"No, Gracie, I am not going to say anything."

"Well anyway—he told me that he was adopted and that he is doing equine therapy. Have you ever heard of that?"

"Yes, I have heard of it."

"He does that stuff with horses, but he also takes riding lessons up at Hawthorne Stables. Did you know that it's right down the road? I walked there yesterday before dinner and saw Andy riding. It looked like lots of fun and I think I would like to take lessons."

I stopped setting the table and waited to see Mom's reaction. She had to think for a minute as she was slicing potatoes.

"Let's ask your father when he comes home."

Just then, Nate blew in the door.

"Hey, what are you all talking about?"

I wasn't quite ready to have Nate be all down on the idea, but Mom spilled it anyway.

"Grace wants to take horseback riding lessons at Hawthorne Stables, which is just up the road."

"What? Where did this even come from?" Nate grinned at me while picking all the carrots out of the salad and eating them.

I grabbed the bowl away from him and put it on the table and wrinkled my nose announcing, "You smell. Maybe you should get a quick shower before dinner."

"I will have you know that I already showered at school."

"Well then, there must be leftover BO on your shirt."

Mom cut into our brother-sister chat. "Nate, Grace is right, go put on a fresh shirt. Dinner's almost ready."

Dad came home and we sat down to eat with Nate joining us smelling better. When I started to clear the table, Mom announced my request and story about meeting Andy during his riding lesson. I could tell she was trying to say just the right thing. Dad's response was typical.

"Nate has some big games coming up. Let's not make any family decisions right now."

I didn't understand why Nate's game schedule had anything to do with me, but I went upstairs to work it all out in my journal. After I settled on my bed and started to write, Nate came in without knocking to ask for help with a book report. What a pain in my butt.

Was I keeping this monster alive by continuing to help him?

Don't answer that.

22. Andy Has a Question

In the two weeks since the last football game, Andy and I ate lunch together every day. He told me more stories about Clyde and his first ever horse show (he didn't win a ribbon). We also liked the same type of music and traded playlists on our phones. I had a few chill lists for when I was reading and writing letters. Andy shared country music that I had never heard, which was wild. Neither of us ever went to any kind of concert except with our parents, and we both agreed that didn't count.

When I got out of the car on Friday morning, Mom said, "Dad and I are driving over to the game at around six o'clock. We might not make it to the pep rally."

"That's okay, I don't need to go. I'll just come home with you at the regular time today after class."

The home football game seemed to have the whole school buzzing. I could tell Nate was preoccupied at breakfast, but he did stop chewing long enough to ask if I would be getting my cowgirl outfit soon. He knew I had gone to Hawthorne Stables to watch Andy and the class again. I ignored Nate and asked about his book report. That shut him up. It was good to see him sweat at something else besides football. Besides, it's English riding with very proper rules and clothes. It isn't the Wild West.

Andy and I sat together again at lunch. He picked a table in the corner of the cafeteria. "I have a question for you," he said in a soft voice, like he was afraid that someone might hear.

"Sure," I said, half expecting him to ask me to do his book report too. Nate had me in a sour mood because he was taking up every bit of room in our house. Maybe someday I'll be center stage in the family.

We unpacked our sandwiches and Andy looked around to see who was sitting near us. He lowered his head a bit and started whispering.

"Grace, I know we've not known each other very long, but I have a special favor to ask you. It's kind of a weird situation, but I trust you and hope that you'll help me."

I didn't know what to think. Andy was folding his napkin into a tiny triangle and wouldn't look at me. "What is it, Andy? You look kind of sad."

He stopped fidgeting with his napkin and looked right at me. "I want to search for my biological mother and I'm wondering if you'll help me."

"What?" I said too loudly and he immediately shushed me. "How come you don't know that already? Can't your parents just tell you?"

"No. Apparently they agreed to some sort of private adoption arrangement, which doesn't help me at all. That should be illegal. Anyway, my mom and dad know I've been thinking about it and honestly, it's probably the reason they suggested equine therapy. They were desperate to distract me."

"But you said you love riding Clyde."

"I do, but that doesn't change the fact that I have all these questions about myself, wondering 'Who am I and where do I come from? Why do I have curly hair?' Hey, I get it that families are not exactly perfect. As far as mine goes, it's great, but I still don't know anything about my roots, my history. What if I have a deadly disease or something?"

"Your parents would've told you, wouldn't they?"

"Maybe they don't know either! But you can help me find out!" Andy unwrapped his lunch carefully and put each item in front of him like pieces on a board game. He picked up a smelly baloney sandwich and heaved a great sigh. Then he looked at me. "You are way smart and know a lot about computer searches. You're like a genius at it, always getting A's. It won't take long, I promise. Plus, I don't want to do the work on my laptop at home, because my parents might see it. They would be crushed if they knew I was doing this."

"I'm sure they would understand. It's only natural that you want to find out more about yourself."

"I've brought it up a few times, but my mom just brushes it off, saying I have plenty of time to do that later. But it's right now that I'm feeling anxious and lonely with a ton of questions. I don't want to hurt my parents. I don't want them to hate me, or worse … leave me."

Andy looked like he was about to cry, but then took a big bite of his sandwich and was suddenly determined saying, "I have to know my story."

"Oh, Andy. Your parents are never going to leave. That's just not going to happen."

"Does that mean you think I'm an idiot and won't help me?"

"Of course not. I would never think you're an idiot, but this means that I have to keep your search a secret from my parents too. It seems very natural to me that you want to discover all you can about your biological mother—is that how you refer to her?"

"Yes. Or, my first mom."

"Does anyone else at school know about this?"

"No, maybe some people know I am adopted, but I'm only telling you this now because we're friends. It's been a while since I had a friend to talk to."

"What am I supposed to tell my parents?" I fidgeted with the rest of my lunch. "Let me think about it. It's another secret on top of the ones I'm already keeping."

"What do you mean? What other secrets are you keeping?"

"I'll tell you later. It's nothing bad, just the normal family drama."

Andy sighed again and put his head on the table for a moment. When he looked up at me, his eyes looked tired, sad, and were getting watery.

I put my hand on his arm. "Please don't be sad. I do want to help and I'm very good at keeping secrets. But this one is serious."

He perked up. "How about if next week we go to the library together? I can work on one of the computers there and you can use your laptop."

The five-minute warning bell rang. We both had to finish our lunch quickly, and there was no time for more talking.

23. Grammy

Mom left school a bit early, so I had to take the bus home anyway, which was no big deal except I always ended up sitting by myself. Today, I had a smile on my face because of Andy. He wanted to do something together with me and that was cool. Still, I just didn't know if I wanted to do it.

When I opened the front door, I heard a familiar voice coming from the kitchen.

"Grammy Ollie!" I shouted and ran to give her a big hug.

"Hello, my dear. How is life in Chicago?"

"It's fine. I'm guessing you're here for the big game?"

"Yes, your father picked me up from the airport earlier this afternoon."

"Are you going to stay the whole weekend?"

"Yes, we will definitely be catching up later. I want you to tell me all about your new school."

Grammy Ollie looked like someone from one of my "senior dwelling" websites where they're trying to get cool old folks to sign up. The slip-on sneakers and sweater set were a dead giveaway. Her hair was a silver teapot shade of gray, not ghost white, and was cut short, but not too-old-to-bother short.

Now that I am writing letters to seniors, I'm a lot more observant. Grammy was certainly in better shape than Mildred. I bet they could be friends though.

I checked to see if she was wearing my favorite ring. For as long as I can remember, Grammy wore an unusual ring on her right hand that was a clock, a timepiece ... a watch on a ring. How do I even describe it? She said it was a gift from "my Bill"—my grandfather. I never met him, but her face lit up whenever she would say his name. It was clear she had married her best friend. I wanted that. Eventually.

We hugged and I pulled out her hand to check.

She threw back her head and laughed. "Yes, it's still ticking. I don't know why you are so fascinated by this thing."

I didn't have a response except that it was such an odd piece of jewelry, especially for someone who didn't give a hoot about the time. Plus, I loved watching her get mushy.

"You can have it when I am pushing up daisies." Grammy loved that phrase and used it often to remind us about her time left on Earth. It always made me laugh because one of the many things Grammy would never be caught dead doing was gardening. In any form.

Mom was at the stove. "Grace, please set the table. We'll have an early dinner and then head over to the field. We don't want to miss the kickoff."

"I hear you are thinking about taking riding lessons." Grammy was fishing for more information about the lessons and about Andy. I was happy to tell her about it.

"Yes, at Hawthorne Stables, and it's practically right down the street. A friend of mine is already taking lessons there and I want to join that class."

It felt good to say, "a friend," but when I thought of him my chest got tight. I was nervous that I would spill Andy's beans. Worse, he had asked me to do something that I was not crazy about.

"Oh, well that's exciting. I didn't know you even liked horses."

"Well, I really don't know much about the whole horse thing. But the animals are beautiful, and I think it would be fun to learn."

"Grace, why don't you go up and change before dinner so we're all ready to leave for the game?"

Mom was stirring something very fast on the stove. It looked like the discussion was over. I was sort of glad not to provide any additional details to Grammy, plus I thought they wanted to get rid of me, so I went halfway up the stairs to listen.

Grammy started with, "Lisa, you look sour about all this horse business. Why don't you just say yes? She made a friend and wants to get out and exercise like you are always nagging her to do."

"Mom, c'mon. Riding horses? Is that even exercise? Besides, don't you need a lot of stuff to ride horses, like the right pants, boots, a helmet? And who knows how much these lessons cost! And then this Andy student that she has met. He has a lot on his mind, trust me." She lowered her voice to a murmur. "I heard that he's trying to work out a few personal issues, and Grace does not need to be part of that."

I ran the rest of the way upstairs to my room. Mildred will be glad to hear from me and I liked the idea of keeping my Chicago senior connection.

Hello Mildred,

It's me, Grace, again. I wrote to you last week but decided that I had a few more things to ask you about making friends at my new school.

A very nice boy, not a boyfriend or anything like that, who takes horseback riding lessons, wants me to join his class. But he has also asked me to help him with a secret research project.

My mom is not sure she wants me to take riding lessons. It's not the right kind of exercise according to her. Can you imagine what she would say about his research project? I haven't decided whether to help him.

I'm finding out that trying to be a good friend and trying to be a good daughter are similar. People want you to do what THEY want you to do and act the way THEY want you to act and if you do those things or act a certain way, then everything is okay. If you don't want to do those things or act in the way they expect, then be prepared to be lonely.

I bet you had good friends and not such good friends. What are some of the things people liked about you? Why is it so hard to make friends?

Your pen pal, Grace Elizabeth

24. Football

On the way to the game, Mom and Dad explained Nate's role on the bench. The school has lots of good players so it made sense that he only played when there was a tremendous lead. He was also able to play in the junior varsity games, which were scheduled the next day. Nate seemed to like those—however, he was only allowed to play if he wasn't used at all in the varsity game. He tended to get super grouchy if he only played one varsity minute and then wasn't allowed to play JV.

"How am I supposed to get any practice if I can't play?"

I didn't know what the answer was because I usually stopped listening to his whining. He should've picked another sport if he wanted to be guaranteed playing time.

There were a bunch of girls hanging by the bench, including PB&J. Nate had no interest in anyone from middle school so that was at least satisfying to me. Did he have a girlfriend? I didn't know. He seemed to only have time for the guys on the team.

It was after halftime when I finally spotted Andy. He was sitting with two older people that were probably his parents. No other kids from our grade were near him. Just like me. Were we both losers in the friend department? I went to get popcorn and could see him waving at me. I waved back. By the time I got back to my seat, we were ahead by a lot. Nate was subbed into the game and caught another pass. Mom, Dad, and Grammy were jumping up and down in the stands. I love my brother—even if I never tell him that—and of course was thrilled for him.

On the car ride home, Grammy announced out of nowhere, "Gracie, how about we go shopping tomorrow for those riding clothes and boots?"

I almost choked on the hard last bits of popcorn in my snack bag. "Awesome! That would be great. Mom, are you okay with this?"

Mom turned to us in the back seat. "Well, you may be jumping the gun just a tad. I haven't even spoken to Chris yet. Is that her name? Horseback riding can be dangerous. What if you fall? How do you know you even like horses?"

"Yes, Chris is the riding instructor, and she told me to come back."

Mom had the final word on everything kid-related. I prepared myself for a letdown.

Grammy interjected, "Lisa, this isn't the time to psychoanalyze everything. The kid wants to ride a horse, what's the big deal?" That seemed to zip up the arguments. Mom turned back around without a word, but I could tell she was mad.

Dad, always a bit late to the party, looked at me in the rearview mirror and smiled. "What's happening now? Is this going to cost a lot?" But he said it with a smile on his face, so I knew he was kidding.

Grammy spoke up right away. "This will be my treat to Gracie, my favorite granddaughter."

"You mean your only granddaughter," Mom always corrected.

"Well, that too." I giggled. I couldn't remember the last time we did something together. This was going to be fun.

Grammy started laughing. "The only thing I know about horses is horse racing. I used to go to a racetrack in Jersey and bet on the ponies. Gosh, that was exciting." Mom and Dad looked at each other while Grammy talked to herself, staring out the window. She added, "Grace, you are probably great with tech stuff. Is there a way I can bet on horses with my phone?"

I gave Grammy a shrug because this was something I knew zero about.

Grammy started scrolling on her phone like she was stabbing a hot potato. For a senior, she had a lot of energy. Finally, she muttered, "What's the name of that darn app again?"

We pulled up in the driveway and Grammy was in a rush to change into her "loungewear." Mom and Dad went into the kitchen for a parent huddle. I crouched on the stairs again out of sight as they processed the night. I was hoping not to hear anything that would squash our shopping plans. Nate's football friends dropped him off in the driveway and I ran upstairs as he came through the front door. The last thing I heard before I closed my bedroom door was Dad saying, "She has outlived two husbands, she can do what she wants with her money. Let her spend some on Gracie."

I couldn't agree more.

25. Chicago Shopping

Dad offered to drive us to the mall or to downtown. Grammy yelled, "Downtown! It's more fun in the city."

The plan was for Dad to drop us off right on North Michigan Avenue. Because we were supposed to take the train back later, he drove to the station first so Grammy knew where it was for the return trip. Then he doubled back for our shopping adventure.

"Now George, don't be a nervous Nelly. Gracie and I will grab a cab back to Union Station and you can pick us up in Oak View on the Red Line. I will text you when we are on the train. We'll be fine."

"Ollie, please call me if you have any issues."

"Will do!" Grammy slammed the car door and put her arm around me as we headed off into the Chicago sunshine.

Our first stop was a beautiful shop with all kinds of boots and riding equipment. I didn't even know the name of the store because I was so overwhelmed. Everything looked prim and proper, but I had my eye on some brown boots that looked just like what the other girls in the class were wearing.

"We'll take them," Grammy said as I clopped up and down the shoe department aisle. It took a bit more time to get the right pants, which are called jodhpurs. Isn't that a funny name? Plus, I tried on many helmets. By the time we finished, Grammy said, "I'm starving!"

At lunch, I ordered iced tea, and Grammy said she deserved a beer. Taking her first sip, she asked, "How do you like your new home and school so far?" She still had a bit of beer foam on her upper lip, and I started to giggle. I picked up my napkin and pointed. She laughed.

"It's fine, I guess. It's been hard to make friends. That's why I wanted to take the riding lessons. Horses are such smart animals; I think I could learn a lot from them. Plus, I already know one boy who's taking lessons."

"A boy?" Grammy was intrigued.

"Not like a boyfriend, just someone who is in my homeroom."

"Makes perfect sense to me." Grammy was nodding now. "Seems like Nate takes up an awful lot of energy in that house and you should have your own thing."

"Yeah, sometimes it bugs me and makes me think there's room for only one star in the family."

"Nonsense." Grammy pounded her hand on the table. "You do whatever you want. You are going to take the riding lessons and be great. Today is all about you. I think you need some new clothes too."

We hit more stores on Lake Shore Drive. Grammy paid for everything, telling me that the money came from her Pennsylvania Lottery winnings. She swore me to secrecy and said that she liked Pick 3 when she remembered to play.

"It used to be called The Daily Number, now it's called Pick 3. I love to play your birthday, February 11. So, I play 2-1-1 and guess what? Last week, I won! I also play your mom's birthday, that's a Pick 4 and other friends' birthdays. Look, here are all the games, but I am still learning about them. There are new ones all the time."

She was scrolling like a crazy person on her phone showing me the different lottery games. Grammy added, "I usually go to a newsstand right around the corner, but I've heard that for the big games like Mega Millions, you can purchase tickets online. Do you think you can help me?" She continued to scroll super-fast and looked like a pro to me. Once in a while, her phone dinged with a reminder of some sort or maybe big buck winnings. I wasn't sure.

By the time we were on the 'L' train, I knew I didn't need to worry about Grammy's savings.

"Grammy, I hope you are not using up all of your savings on these games."

"No, I'm pretty conservative with my money. Don't worry. I set a limit each month for my lottery activities. Remember, they benefit senior citizens!"

With half an eye on me and half on the phone, she continued, "I think I told you about the ladies in my birthday group?" I nodded. "Once a month, we get together and celebrate all the birthdays in that month. After cake and ice cream, we usually play bridge. It's unbelievably boring—I could scream."

"What kind of excitement are you looking for?"

"Well, it started with church bingo. I've been playing that for years and loved the group fun, the chocolate cake, the punch." She winked at me. I was confused. "You know, the punch—always spiked with something delicious. Anyway, it was enjoyable, but everyone is old and frail. I wanted to mix it up, so I convinced my friend Carol to take one of those bargain buses to the Atlantic City casinos that I used to do with Bill. Carol and I are trying to learn some new games together. Her grandson showed us how to search for anything on YouTube and now I am fascinated by all the videos. Here, take a look."

She swiped and tapped, and I saw, "How to Play Blackjack for Beginners."

Grammy smiled, showing a smidge of lipstick on her teeth. "See? Everything can be learned via YouTube video. I am learning all the blackjack tricks of the trade."

I made a mental note to research what YouTube videos were available for finding friends.

26. Yarn

Grammy surprised me again when we got home. After dinner she said, "I have something to show you."

I wondered what other amazing things could possibly be shared today. The guest room was a bit of a mess. Mom and Dad tried to share the space as an office, but there was just not enough room for two people's worth of stuff. The full-sized bed made the room cramped. Out-of-season clothes were stacked in laundry baskets. Grammy's bottles, creams, and jewelry covered the dresser.

Grammy didn't seem to mind or care and was set up with her own nest of pillows and blankets, digging through her carry-on bag. "Sit here," she said, patting the edge of the bed next to her. In the duffel were several balls of yarn, all shades of blue, my favorite color. "I figured that you painted your new room blue, and I was right."

Smiling now, I started to examine all the pretty wool skeins. Some were wound in balls; others still had the paper labels from the store around them.

As long as I can remember, Grammy was a needlework whiz and never even used a pattern. She made the afghan on my bed, stitching at least a dozen different kinds of granny squares. If it could be made with a crochet hook, Grammy would figure it out.

My personal handmade Grammy collection included a constant supply of pink slippers, multicolored scarves with matching mittens, and tiny dresses for my dolls. The slippers needed to be worn with socks for maximum warmth, and they were slippery on hardwood floors, but they were perfect when I didn't want to wear shoes around the house. The crowning touch was a pink pom-pom ball on the top of my toes. About twice a year, I would get a new pair because my feet were growing unusually fast.

Grammy had already started on a new granny square color combination for me. The blue squares had light shades of green with lavender trim, all my best-loved shades. She pulled out a few squares and laid them side by side on the bed. The way the colors blended together looked like a springtime cloud. She started stitching away at breakneck speed.

"Well, do you like it so far? You are always wrapping yourself up in multiple layers of blankets and quilts. I wanted to make something for you so that you don't forget me."

"Grammy, I love it and will keep it on my bed. And I could never forget you."

"Good. Now look, I brought a larger hook for you to practice. It was in a whole set, so I have plenty. I also have some bright blue yarn for us to begin with a chain stitch. Then we could work on some other stitches. You can make anything with just a few different stitches."

With that, she positioned the hook in my right hand and helped me to move the thread around the index finger on my left hand. The chain stitch was supposed to be a simple grab and pull, all one motion. I was all thumbs and the thread was tangled when Mom came in.

"Time for bed, Grace. You can pick that up tomorrow."

Mom put her hand on my back as I left the room, and I heard her say to Grammy, "Too bad I never had any patience for crocheting."

"Lisa, you just didn't stick with it."

"I didn't make the time for handicrafts once I had studying on my mind. There were more important things to me than making a scarf that I would never wear. Grace is very busy with school, you know. Please don't be upset if she doesn't continue with it."

I could just picture Grammy's face at that moment. Mom has a knack for telling the truth a little too honestly sometimes and that can hurt. Like when our batting cage softball fiasco tested her coaching ability. "Honestly, Grace, it's just simple hand-eye coordination. Can you at least try?" She made it sound like I was purposely messing up. I just couldn't get the hang of it.

Crochet is probably a good hobby for Grammy to relax instead of scrolling for games on her phone. When I went in to say goodnight, she was softly counting out the stitches to start the next color.

"Goodnight, my sweet girl," she said, giving me a big hug. "You do whatever the heck you want to do. Don't worry about me."

27. Goodnight Mildred

I went back to my room feeling like I had to check in with Mildred. The world of adults was confusing sometimes. Will I ever understand what they're thinking, and will they ever understand me?

> *Dear Mildred,*
>
> *Hello and how are you?*
>
> *Did you ever feel like you didn't know your children at all? Sometimes, I wonder what makes people love each other.*
>
> *I love my mom, but sometimes, I don't like her or understand her. It's hard to explain. Family love is hugely important. It's made me who I am, but at the same time, I can see how family love can hurt and disappoint. I love each family member a little bit differently.*
>
> *Do you think that is okay?*

Maybe that's why I am still looking for friends. Family can be friends, but it's important to be with friends your own age. I just have not found that person yet. I will keep looking.

The boy that I have met, Andy, is the closest thing I have had to a friend in a while. I am hoping he still likes me after our secret mission is over.

Let me know what you think.

Your friend and pen pal,

Grace Elizabeth

28. Church

On Sunday, surprise! Mom announced we were going to church as soon as we woke up. To be honest, I had almost forgotten about it. We've only been there once since moving to Chicago. There was an actual choir, although we still didn't sing all the verses to the songs. Maybe that's a Catholic thing. Since I did not have Jeez classes to go to, Mom and Dad dropped church the ball. Honestly, Nate and I did not mind too much. We had other things to do.

There was one smiling face in the pew though—Grammy. She brought out her rosary and prayed up a storm all through Mass. I never understood that. Why do double duty? You are already getting Catholic credit for being at Mass, why pile on with the prayers? It seemed unnecessary.

Thankfully, the sermon was short, and before I knew it, we were going with God out the door. Grammy at least waited that long to begin with the questions.

"Do you like your new church?" Grammy asked no one from the back seat of the car.

Mom jumped in right away, "Honestly the kids have a lot going on—we haven't had much of a chance to go."

"How will the children make up their minds about religion if you don't go to church?"

The question hung in the air for a moment—we didn't know what to say. Mom seemed reluctant to get into an argument with Grammy. So that's where we left it.

29. Grammy Love

It was Monday morning before I knew it. I think I fell asleep at my desk but woke up in my bed. At breakfast, Dad said he would drive Grammy to the airport. I didn't think she would be up early to say goodbye, but when I finished my cereal, she was downstairs, lipstick and all, ready to go.

"Mother, are you sure I can't fix you an egg or something? Aren't you hungry this morning?"

Mom never made anyone breakfast, so I wasn't sure how that was going to happen. Grammy was quick to read the sitch and didn't miss a beat.

"No, I will get something at the airport." She turned to me. "Now, you can call me anytime, remember that." Grammy whispered as she gave me a hug. "And don't forget to practice your chain stitch."

"I'll try, Grammy. And you hold on to your money."

"I told you, I am learning some new games and should have a foolproof system soon," she said, winking at me. Dad's eyes rolled back in his head. Mom held Grammy's carry-on bag, shifting from one foot to the other. Nate came running down the stairs with his gym bag. The smell filled the hallway. Were there dirty socks in there ... or worse?

Nate notified us all in a matter-of-fact tone, "Another guy from the team is picking me up in ten minutes. Is there any cereal left?" He gave Grammy a quick peck on the cheek and started pouring from all the boxes on the counter.

Mom called back into the kitchen, "Plenty of cereal. You're on your own to lock up, since we're all leaving now. Let's not make anyone late today." Mom made these pronouncements like a school crossing guard. I was surprised she wasn't hand signaling Grammy to the car.

Grammy knew her daughter. "Don't fret, Lisa, I will be out of your hair in a minute. Just saying goodbye to my favorite granddaughter."

"Your only granddaughter!" we all hollered together.

"Send me a picture of you on the horse," Grammy yelled as she eased into the car butt-first.

"I will!" I shouted back, blowing her a kiss.

Watching Grammy get smaller as Dad's car went out of sight, I was suddenly sad. But knowing that I had asked Mildred about family love and friends made me happy. What a confusing topic. I held out hope that she would help me figure it all out.

Standing there, I remembered that I left Mildred's letter out in the open on my desk. I raced upstairs, added a few heart stickers, and then dug around in my drawer for an envelope. Mom was beeping the horn impatiently as I looked for a stamp.

I found one in the office desk, thank goodness. I was out of breath by the time I slammed the car door. "Mom, I have a letter to send to Connie. Can you stop at the mailbox at the end of the block so I can drop it in?"

"Sure, honey. Oh, I'm pleased that you're writing to Connie."

I felt bad about lying, but didn't want to explain my Mildred letters to mom. Maybe I'll never hear back from Mildred, but it made me feel better to ask the questions. I will write to Connie at some point. Doesn't everyone deserve a second chance?

30. Andy Is Waiting

During homeroom, Andy kept looking over at me like he was expecting a thumbs-up. I still had too many questions. How was this my problem to solve? Isn't this something for Andy to work out with his parents? It wasn't until after our first period with Ms. Infante that we were able to talk.

"Grace, were you able to think about what I said last week? Will you help me look for my birth mother?"

"I don't know, Andy. It would be nice to help you, but I don't know anything about this. Are you sure you just don't want to talk to your mom or dad?"

"I can't hurt their feelings. If we do this in secret, then no one is mad at me."

"But don't you think they'll find out?"

"No, the fact that my birth mother wanted a private adoption tells me everything. She doesn't want anyone to know. But if I find out who she is, then I know who I'm connected to."

"Why is that so important?" I asked. We were walking back to our homeroom.

"Because I don't look like anyone. You are the spitting image of your mom."

"I am nothing like her."

"No, I don't mean similar in personality. You look like her. I bet people always tell you that. You know that you belong to her. You're both tall with the same wavy hair and freckles. When I go out with my parents, people stare and wonder where I came from."

"Now you know that's not exactly true. Your mom and dad love you. You're thinking that everyone is staring at you, but that's not happening. Do random people really care?"

Andy was stubborn and wouldn't give up. "I care, and I am sure everyone knows."

"Trust me, no one cares. Yes, I look like my mom with curly hair that never stays in place, freakishly long legs and arms, and eyes that need glasses like my dad to see the SMART Board. It's every girl's dream."

"You don't get it. Try to understand where I'm coming from. There are things that my parents do that drive me crazy. My father is the life of the party.

He loves to tell jokes and has a million stories about growing up in a small town in Michigan, then going to the University of Chicago. He was president of his frat and played lacrosse. Mom looks like everyone's best friend. She used to be a nurse, and now does some sort of medical consulting. At night she's taking grad school courses. Meanwhile, I am antisocial. I hate being with people and can't seem to concentrate on anything. That's why I get along with horses. There isn't a medical bone in my body. I fell off my bike the other day and almost threw up when I saw blood."

At that, I started to giggle.

"Grace, it's not funny. I desperately need your help to solve this. I can tell from the books you read and the fact that you love to write, you would be super good at helping me research this."

"Andy, I think you're overestimating me. I don't have any special skills."

"Well, you've been a good listener and didn't make fun of me for being in equine therapy."

We picked up our backpacks and headed to the cafeteria for lunch. Andy looked dejected. I weighed the reasons out in my head. Did I want to do this? It wasn't as if the rest of the girls were knocking at my door to sit with me or invite me to their houses for sleepovers. Andy had his sad puppy-dog face on again. After buying drinks, we sat down in a corner by ourselves.

"Okay, I will help you, but with the search part of it only. If there are any emails or phone calls needed, that will be all you."

Andy broke out into a huge grin. He looked sort of goofy when he smiled extra wide. Then he threw back his head and laughed big—Connie style. For a second, I thought of our friendship and missed it.

"Oh, Grace, this is great. You're sure? Oh, fantastic. It's going to be a fun adventure, you'll see."

I didn't tell Andy, but there was another reason I said yes. First thing that morning, I saw Patty from the PB&J mean trio. Her locker was near mine and she came over and said, not even in a low voice, "I see you're hanging out with that weirdo Andy. I heard from some of the other kids that he has a few problems." She paused to emphasize the word "problems."

"I don't know what you are talking about," I said, slamming my locker way harder than I needed to. Patty jumped. "He's very nice, and I like hanging out with him." I couldn't think of anything else to say until later of course. Who was she to talk about weird?

31. Mr. J's Essay Contest

Mr. J began the class with his usual enthusiasm, rocking forward on his tip toes as he shouted. "How's everybody doing?"

Total silence.

The period right before Mr. J was math with Ms. Infante, which was why we were all a little brain-dead.

"Okay, everybody up!" Mr. J commanded. He then proceeded to give stretching commands: arm circles, reach overhead, touch your back, and so on. When we were all sufficiently giggling and woken up, he turned on the SMART Board which read:

Essay Contest Rules

Mr. J announced that the best way to practice our writing was to write! The eighth graders would be writing short stories, but for now, our first writing assignment would be a personal essay.

"Don't worry about the contest now. We'll have plenty of time to practice with shorter essays and to experiment with different topics. But this is what we are working toward." Mr. J continued, "Some of the same elements of storytelling could be applied to essay writing. This is an excellent first step to improve your writing."

Seventh Grade
Fall Essay Contest Rules
Mr. Curtis Janowski
Room 7-J

1. Essays must be 500-700 words

2. Essays must address one of the contest topics.* Topic and outline due on Wednesday before Thanksgiving.

3. Essays must be the original work of the student. Plagiarism of any kind including using the work of another student, or any form of AI will result in disqualification.

4. Essays must be in 12-pt Times New Roman font, double spaced. Submit to CJanowski@oakview.edu by December 15.

5. Essays should demonstrate proper grammar, punctuation, and spelling appropriate for seventh grade. Proofread your work!

6. Essays will be judged on creativity, clarity of expression, organization of ideas and overall effectiveness of communication.

7. The Essay Contest is open to all SEVENTH-grade students at Oak View School.

*The following are suggestions for essay topics:
- The Importance of Kindness
- The Meaning of Friendship
- My Role Model
- My favorite book or movie
- Overcoming Challenges
- Pick Your Own Topic (to be approved by Mr. J)

It's going to be painfully hard to pick from this list. I started to scribble ideas in my notebook.

"Don't worry about choosing a topic for the fall contest right now," Mr. J assured us. "We'll start with a topic very familiar to you for practice—not these topics. For your preliminary essay, I am asking for three hundred words just to get a feel for self-expression. After that, you will work up to the five-to-seven-hundred-word piece for the fall contest which won't be due until mid-December. How does that sound?"

Before anyone could respond Mr. J continued, "We will all have the same topic to start with for this first essay. The holiday season is fast approaching. I'd like everyone to write three hundred words on family traditions during the holidays. That's a good topic for your first attempt, right?" Mr. J flipped to the next slide on the SMART Board.

Current assignment:
Holiday Family Traditions: 300 words
Due: November 15

Mr. J started to break down the different sections of our essay: introduction, body paragraphs, and information to support a conclusion. We also talked about the importance of a good opening sentence to get the reader's attention. I knew some of this stuff already but was excited to begin writing. There is only so much I can say in my journal … and to Mildred.

32. Two Heads are Better Than One

At the end of the day, Andy waited for me in the hall.

"Are you ready to start working on our project? We have to give ourselves a name."

"What? Why? That sounds like something little kids do. You're acting like we're Spy Kids or something."

"Grace, this is important. What if we have to talk about this in front of people? We don't want to give it away."

"Why would we even need to do that?" We were two minutes into "our project" and Andy was already getting on my nerves. Was I going to regret this?

"You are not taking this seriously," Andy said with a pout face.

OMG! I could tell he was mad now. Was the anger always there? What if we didn't succeed? Would he blame me?

Andy followed me out of school and wouldn't stop talking. "Listen, I have a great idea. My parents never miss a University of Chicago alumni meeting. They met there when they were juniors, and once a month, they get together with friends for drinks or go to some event. Sometimes they come over to our house. You should hear the stories."

"So, what does that have to do with us?"

"Sooooo …," Andy continued, but I could tell he was getting impatient. "They are out for hours on that night. I think the date is coming up. There's a huge box in their bedroom closet that says ADOPTION. I thought the first thing we could do would be to go through that box and see if we find any juicy secrets."

"Actually, I was thinking of a better plan. Why don't you come over to my house first? We could work on my computer and plan out what we're going to do because we have no idea how to go about this."

"I guess I was just super anxious to dive right in." Andy hung his head. "Grace, I don't think you understand what this means to me."

"Andy, I think I do. Listen, you trusted me enough to tell me about equine therapy. Honestly, I need time to work up to sneaking into your parents' closet. Let's take one step at a time."

"Okay, we can do it your way."

Andy started to walk away, toward the car pickup lane. Even with my terrible math skills, I was able to count twelve weeks in this new town with only one friend to show for it. I ran after him.

"Andy, wait. You have my word that I'll do everything I can to help. Let's go to my house and decide what to do next."

He didn't say anything, but I could tell he was a little ticked. "My mom's pulling up," he said. "Wanna ride?"

His mom, Beth, was pretty and petite. Her light brown hair was pulled back into a stylish twist. She probably just finished a barre class in her deep maroon yoga pants and matching jacket.

"Hi Mom, this is Grace. Can you drop us at her house? We have a homework project."

"It's so nice to meet you, Grace."

It took only a few minutes before we pulled into my driveway. Mrs. Cassidy burst out laughing. "Gone Away Court! What an interesting address."

Mom came to the door and was surprised but broke into a smile. She waved to Mrs. Cassidy and held the door open for us. "Hello Andy, I finally get to meet the person who inspired Grace to be a horsewoman. Are you two studying together?"

Mom turned to busy herself tidying up the kitchen and I mouthed "relax" to Andy while making a slowdown motion with my hands. I'm not normally a bossy girl, but I had to step in or Andy's weirdness in the moment would have Mom asking more questions.

"Yes, thank you. I think Grace is going to like it—the horseback riding lessons I mean," he said, trying to act all nonchalant but he was flustered and failing. I was trying not to laugh.

"What are you two cooking up today?" Mom was probably dying of curiosity as she started to gather the junk mail from the kitchen table.

I jumped in because Andy immediately looked guilty. "We have a book report due and thought we would trade ideas about the story."

"Oh, that's great, I'll be happy to read it later," Mom said as she zipped up her computer bag. I felt terrible lying right to Mom's face.

She went upstairs to her office, which left Andy and me to whisper argue.

"She's going to hear us." His face scrunched in worry.

"No, she gets absorbed in her own stuff, plus she's on the phone a lot. Let's eat junk food and drink milk. Go look in the cabinet above the oven and I'll see what I can find on Google."

Andy grabbed the orange ginger snap box and held it up, victorious. He started eating cookies like he was starving.

"Slow down. Get something to drink, come over here and look at my search results. I just searched for Illinois adoption laws and nothing much can happen until you are eighteen."

Andy moved on to pretzels and started talking and crunching. It was not a good look. Between swallows he sputtered, "But if we find the smoking gun in the adoption box at my house, that doesn't matter."

"Andy, this isn't CSI. Even if we find something, how are two twelve-year-olds going to make anything happen?"

"For someone named Grace, you have zero faith. I am sure if I find her and call her, she'll want to meet me."

"You don't know that for sure. I just don't want you to be disappointed."

His eyes told me everything I needed to know. "It's always the little things that I notice. When we get together with my cousins, they have the same mannerisms, the same laugh, the way they move. I feel like a weirdo next to them. I've told you before, I am desperate to find my connection."

"Are you sure you're not just picking up on these things because you're adopted?"

"It's hard to explain. I love animals of all kinds and have been begging my mom for a dog. Another therapist I was seeing recommended equine therapy and it's been good for me. My mom thought it was a bit silly and my dad is grossed out by animals of all kinds. He said, 'How can you stand the smell?'"

"Well," I offered, "if they hated it, you wouldn't be allowed to go."

"That's true."

Andy was counting on me to help find answers about his birth mom and I was more unsure than ever.

Time to rely on the reliable. Maybe Mildred could help me sort it out.

33. Mildred Learns About KISSS

Dear Mildred,

Hello and how are you? Writing to you about what's happening in my life makes me feel better. I don't expect to hear back from you, but it helps me to put my thoughts down on paper.

I hope that's okay with you.

I have myself in a bit of a pickle, as my Grammy always says. My friend Andy, who is adopted, is looking to find his birth mom. He has asked me for help and this whole adventure is becoming very tricky. First, we have to lie about what we are doing, since no one can find out. Then I don't even know if I am going to be able to help him.

Is that crazy or what? He loves his mom and dad, but this is just something he has to do.

When I Google "adoption in Illinois," everything says that we are too young to look at birth records.

Andy is very determined and I think I understand why. He even wants to "name" this project of ours. We are on a mission to find his biological mother—but Bio Mission or Bio Mother—both have BM as initials and that's not going to work for obvious reasons! I am going to suggest that we call our project KISSS: Kids in Search of Something Secret. Let's see what Andy thinks of that.

I hope you've made some nice friends where you are and they're not getting you into trouble!

Your pen pal friend,

Grace Elizabeth

34. Tied to Family

Even Mildred can't help me with Nate's book report. That's just a fact. The report is due tomorrow, but luckily, nerd that I am, I read *The Hunger Games* last year. When I mentioned to Nate that he would love the book, he ignored me and streamed it instead.

Nate said that most of his friends already read the book and he wanted my report so he could talk to them before class. He needed to answer a few questions around characters and themes. I was fresh off my session with Andy so thinking about family obligations was definitely on my mind. It didn't take long—I made a few notes and dropped it on his desk.

"Thanks dingus." He never tired of calling me that. "It looks a bit skimpy. Is this it?"

"Yep, time to suck it up and do some work, buddy."

Helping Nate write a report is stupendously easier than an actual "hunger game." At least I didn't have to kill off the rest of the football team to do it. In *The Hunger Games*, Katniss risked everything for her sister. Nate wouldn't even share his popcorn on family movie night.

Andy doesn't have a sibling. Would that help if he did? I don't know.

Being connected to my family is something I don't really think about. Nate and I are obviously different, but the fact that we're siblings creates a kind of invisible thread. It's like Grammy's crochet yarn and the chain stitch we practiced together. The chain is the Mackenzie family, and even though Nate is a crummy brother, he's still my brother. We're from the same skein, the same ball of yarn tied to our parents. Yes, I may have small boobs and curly hair, but that connected me in a special way to my mom.

What did it feel like to be adopted and not have that connection? What did it feel like to be called a family and not be a stitch on that chain? Did it feel like a pretend family to Andy?

Mom has told me the story of how I came into the world many times. She had my due date circled in red on the kitchen wall calendar. However, I came a week early, in the middle of the night. The doctor said to get to the hospital right away. Then I took forever to arrive. It was a spring day, but very hot.

The hospital air conditioning was on full blast and Dad joked for years how he was freezing in the delivery room waiting for me. When I was very young, I would ask her to tell me that story over and over.

Andy didn't have a story in the same way that I did. It was starting to dawn on me that nothing we did together—even finding his birth mother—would change that.

Or would it?

35. My First Lesson

Saturday was my first horseback riding lesson. Mrs. Cassidy offered to pick me up because she was already taking Andy to the same class.

"Let's text Grammy a picture," Mom said.

My new riding pants, boots, and helmet looked great, but I felt stupid posing on the front lawn. Maybe it was because I was wearing my new bra for the first time. It was blue decorated with flowers and Mom helped me adjust the straps. Still, it felt weird, and I tried not to concentrate on it. Grammy would be happy to see the result of our shopping efforts, so I smiled and held up my riding crop.

Andy's mom was right on time. "Thank you, Mrs. Cassidy," I said, shutting the back door.

"You are welcome, Grace. It's nice that Andy will know someone in the class now."

Mrs. Cassidy looked picture perfect again today. This time, she was wearing a navy vest over a long sleeve, gray fitted top. Mom came over to say hello and Mrs. Cassidy didn't seem to notice Mom's old sweatpants and one of Dad's fleece jackets.

"Thank you, Beth. I can pick them up at the end of the lesson and drop Andy off at home."

"Great. The lesson is usually an hour with about twenty minutes for the kids to put their gear away."

"This is wonderful," Mom gushed. She seemed happy about the lesson, a bit different from the reaction I heard when she was talking to Grammy.

I was impatient to get going and buckled my seat belt, announcing, "Ready," hoping they would get the hint and go. Andy rolled his eyes at me from the front seat.

It only took a minute to get there.

"I'm nervous," I whispered to Andy as we walked into the barn.

"Don't be. You'll see how nice Chris is."

"Do you know your way around the barn and all the other buildings on the property?"

"It's called a stable," Andy corrected.

Chris came over and before she even spoke was sizing me up. I didn't know where to look.

"Grace, we're glad you're here. Your mom and I spoke on the phone." Stopping in front of one of the stalls she mumbled "Oh, you're tall," more to herself. Then she turned and announced, "Twiggy is the perfect horse for you. She has your long legs and is graceful and beautiful. Let's go over and meet Twiggy."

Andy had started to get Clyde ready for the lesson. I followed Chris into the stall to see a beautiful, black horse with a shiny coat munching on hay. She raised her head to look me over and I put my hand gently on her shoulder like Andy taught me to do.

"Twiggy has just been brushed and is all ready for you. I'll show you how to saddle her up."

We worked together but Chris did most of the actual saddling. Is that even a word? I was trying to understand everything she was saying, but it was being dumped into my brain all at once. Chris wanted me to get used to her, and I gave her oats to eat out of my hand, which tickled like a million wet feathers in my palm. Twiggy probably wanted more oats, I figured. She nuzzled up to me, sort of like giving me a peck on the cheek. Maybe she did want food, but she made me smile. It felt like she was talking to me.

We walked Twiggy around the outside of the riding area. Then Chris showed me the proper way to mount my horse, and away we went toward the ring. I didn't even need help getting my foot in the stirrup. Because it was my first lesson, Chris rode alongside me instead of standing at the center of the ring. "You're doing fine. I can tell Twiggy likes you. We'll take it slow because you need some time to get used to each other."

Twiggy and I stood off to the side while Andy and the other three students started to trot their horses around the ring. Chris explained all about posting. That was all the bouncing up and down I saw earlier but didn't realize it was done on purpose! Twiggy and I mostly walked for the hour, but then tried trotting and posting as best as I could. My coordination was apparently in need of improvement. I kept posting at the wrong time and the saddle was bumping up and hurting my butt with every step. Maybe I just needed to get used to the rhythm. After a while, I felt like I was hanging onto Twiggy for dear life. My beautiful horse seemed to understand and didn't make any sudden movements.

After the lesson, Chris helped me store the saddle, bridle, and everything from our ride. "I like your boots, Grace."

"Oh, thank you. My grandmother helped me pick them out."

"Well, it's important to have the right equipment. But you won't feel at home on Twiggy for a while."

While Andy and I were waiting for my mom, I asked him, "Are you still doing equine therapy?"

Andy grabbed a broom from the front of the stable and began to sweep. "Yes, I like that it's on a different day from riding lessons so I can spend more time with Clyde."

"Is it helping you?"

Andy was sweeping like his life depended on it but stopped to answer my question. "When I take care of Clyde, I am responsible for him. We're joined together. Connected. I understand that he's a horse, but there is something awesomely beautiful about him. We communicate without saying a word. He listens to me, and when I want him to do something, he does it."

After spending just an hour with Twiggy, I sort of got it. She's an amazing, but powerful animal who kissed me.

Andy continued, "You know how when people are old, they get a cat or a dog and it helps them not to feel sad and lonely?"

I thought about Mildred and Betty and other ladies I had written to. Lots of seniors I read about had cats and other animals they loved.

Andy continued, "I even read about a cancer patient who got a puppy to visit him in the hospital. Well, with Clyde, that's the feeling I get when I am with him. He makes me feel better about everything."

"That sounds wonderful." I started to say something about our project, but my mom pulled up in her car and I stopped.

"Well, how was the first lesson, Grace?" Mom was curious. She had changed out of her sweats and wore jeans and her own fleece jacket.

Andy got in the back, and I climbed in the front seat. I made sure to tell my mom the truth. "It was the most fun I've had since moving here."

36. Girlfriends

Andy's project would have to take a little pause because I decided to focus on finding a friend who I could hang out with, preferably a girl. Yes, I would put myself out there. Maybe it was riding Twiggy … or maybe I was just growing up. But I was starting to feel pretty good about myself and was ready for a girlfriend. Plus, I was smarter than I was two months ago. Any girl in my grade who even mentioned Nate was not worth talking to. Our school had lots of activities, and I was determined to find someone that I could laugh with—like Connie. When I thought about the fun times we had, I missed her.

Connie always sat next to me on the bus when we had field trips. There were times in the parking lot waiting for parents to pick us up after Jeez that we would laugh until we were sick. Once in a while, we would have a sleepover and eat way too much popcorn and Twizzlers. We both liked the same junk food.

The good news was that practice had started for the Christmas concert. It was a chance to get to know some girls until I could figure out how to help Andy.

During the month of November until the concert in December, we would be practicing our "holiday medley." It was a fun combination of songs. The chorus included most of the boys and girls in my grade. The kids that actually could sing would be doing solos. Singing was not one of my top talents, but in a chorus, who would hear me?

Charlotte was in the homeroom across the hall. We were both pretty tall and ended up on the top rung of the risers. I called it the geek section, but Charlotte was no geek. Her hair was long and dark brown. Someone at home was extremely talented in the braiding and the whole updo skill set. Some days, her hair was in a simple ponytail that fell down her back and other days, twisted in a French braid with ribbons through it. I was hoping she didn't notice my hair or my singing. Her voice was divine.

One day after chorus, Charlotte and I were walking back to our classrooms and my brain went blank. How do I start a conversation? All of a sudden, before she went into her homeroom, she turned to me and said, "Hey, I heard what Patty, Becky and Janet did at the game. That was really mean. I don't like it when people aren't honest about what they're doing."

"How did you hear about it?"

"Oh, girls talk."

"I don't talk to them anymore, so I hope they're not still talking about me."

"No, I think they've given up." The she changed the subject. "I saw that you were carrying around The Hunger Games. What'd you think of it?"

It turns out Charlotte likes to read! She also seemed nervous talking to me, which I thought was funny. I didn't tell her I helped Nate write his book report, which, by the way, he got an A on. He barely said thank you but told me he would let me know about the next assignment shortly. Thanks, big brother.

The day after choir practice, Charlotte came to sit with Andy and me at lunch. I was so happy, I forgot to eat most of my sandwich and had to take it home. Andy, however, was not as mesmerized by the company. He looked like he had ants in his pants, as Grammy always says. On the way back to homeroom, he whispered, "Meet me in the parking lot after school."

There was no getting around it, so I went. Andy rushed over to me—I'd never seen him that excited. He had a date and time for his parents to be out of the house. "How about we meet next Saturday at my house for K-I-S-S-S? The coast will be clear!"

Oh boy. I started to hum the Mission Impossible movie music ... dum dum da da. Andy walked away shaking his head, but I could see him smiling.

At least he liked our new name.

37. Connie

Connie must have felt her ears twitching, or whatever that saying is. There was another letter from her on the hall table when I got home from school. I wasn't sure how I felt about it.

Mom said, "Well, just open it and see what she has to say."

> *Dear Grace,*
>
> *Who says that all our Jeez training was for nothing? My so-called friends are not friends. I think they didn't like you more than they liked me, if that makes sense. It was more important to them that we not be friends. Now I am wondering what friendship is all about.*
>
> *I only know that I would give anything to be able to laugh again like we did after Jeez classes.*
>
> *What are your new activities at Gone Away Court? Will you ever write to me?*

Let me know about life in the Windy City ... I Googled Chicago and that came up. Is it windy there? Your curly hair must hate that.

Just know that I am sorry for what happened.

Love,

Connie (your former Constant)

Mom was leaning over my shoulder. "Well? What did she say?"

"She's sorry about how we left it." I didn't see the point of going into details. It still stung to have my only friend make a fool of me. But she saw that it was for nothing.

"Maybe she'll make a trip out to Chicago someday."

"Maybe," I smiled as I ran up the stairs. For the first time in forever, I had other possible friends to think about.

I could get used to this.

38. The Adoption Box

Andy had the next Saturday all planned out. Our riding lesson would be in the morning. Then in the afternoon, his parents would be going to their college alumni event. This cleared the way for KISSS. He told me to ride my bike to his house after the lesson and that he'd leave the garage door open for me to pull right in. Incognito style.

Once again, I cracked up. "Andy, can't you just tell your parents that a friend is coming over? Your mother has already met me."

"No, I just don't want to answer any questions."

"Okay, Andy Snickett, let's see what happens."

I didn't have any reason to lie about where I was going, so I told my mom I was riding my bike over to Andy's. Oh wait, I did have to tell a small fib.

"Will Andy's parents be home?" she asked, half distracted looking over leftovers from the fridge. On Saturdays, it seemed like everyone was going in different directions. Food was a bit of a "get your own" situation in our house.

"Oh, yeah. Sure," I yelled halfway out the door.

"Well, maybe they'll want you to stay for dinner."

"Maybe, but I can just grab whatever's leftover when I get home."

"Okay, that's fine."

So far so good. Andy would be happy that no alarm bells were raised with my exit. He needed to calm down.

He met me at the garage door and then hit the automatic closer when I was inside. I forgot how fun it was to ride my bike. Back in Pennsylvania, Connie and I rode bikes together. I thought about her letters. Should I write to her? I stopped myself. There wasn't time to think about that. We had a KISSS case to crack.

Andy's face was birthday-party excited, smiling ear to ear. He was still carrying around his Nancy Drew notebook and scribbling in it as we made our way upstairs. The Cassidy house had a different look than the Mackenzie address, that's for sure. I would call my mom's decorating style somewhat informal, put-your-feet-up casual. The Cassidy look was fancier. Everything went together and sort of matched. Pillows were everywhere. Plus, their house was larger than ours and had more rooms downstairs. There was a game room and then a different room with leather chairs that had cup holders for TV watching. I wanted to look around, but Andy, the newest Hardy boy, was impatient.

"C'mon, Grace. We won't have much time once we get started."

Andy led the way to his parents' bedroom, which I can only describe as beautiful. He picked up a remote control from the dresser and the shades lowered with a click. I wanted to jump on the bed in the middle of the fluffiest comforter I had ever seen, but I controlled myself. We were on a mission, after all.

The walk-in closet was already open. It was huge, with shelves to the ceiling. There was even a step ladder tucked in the corner. Once he climbed up, he slid a box labeled "Adoption" from behind some other shoe boxes and handed it to me.

"How did you even know it was up here?" I asked.

"I've been snooping for a while but never had the nerve to take it off the shelf."

We settled on the floor and opened the lid. Inside were a bunch of folders, loose papers, and a big three-ring binder. I helped him lift out the enormous book.

"I just didn't have the guts to look through any of these things before." Andy looked at me, and I gave him a nod of encouragement.

It felt like the movie *National Treasure* as we pulled precious documents from the box.

I wasn't even sure Andy was listening to me, but the box was a mess, and I was dying to organize it. "Why don't we sort through all the things by date? You know, the papers your parents had to fill out to get approved first, before the adoption. Then, once they were approved, who they contacted. It's all a matter of timing."

"Yeah, sure," he said with his nose in the binder. "Look, here are the pictures they gave to the agency."

I peered over Andy's shoulder to see the ultimate professional couple posing on vacation, plus other photos of family members during various holiday gatherings. The photos of Mr. and Mrs. Cassidy were sweet. You could tell they loved each other.

"Look, here is the home study report," he announced.

"What's that?" I asked.

"It's when the agency comes over to your house to see if it's an okay place to raise a child."

"I'm guessing they passed with flying colors." I picked out another couple of files from the box. "Andy, are you sure you don't want to keep this stuff out and then just talk to your parents about it?"

"No." He was determined. "I don't want them to know I was even looking through their papers."

"Well, they're going to find out sooner or later." Andy wasn't listening to me again. I could see he was absorbed in the enormous data dump of info. There were lots of forms. "What's in there?"

"You wouldn't believe all this crap. Here's a psychological assessment," he said, reading off the first page. "There are also letters of reference, reports on books about adoption, copies of their marriage license, and personal essays."

After he said the word "essays," I lost him for a good five minutes as he read his parents' personal pleading for a child.

"Andy, this feels too personal. I'm not sure I should even be here while you're looking at these things."

"Grace, please stay. We have to find something we can use. But I understand. Everything we're reading is making me depressed."

I dug down to the bottom of the box and pulled out a folder with a label that said, "Birth Certificate." Sure enough, it was Andy's certified birth document, however, it listed Beth and Tom Cassidy as parents.

Andy's shoulders slumped.

"Oh, c'mon. It couldn't have been that easy. We'll keep looking," I said in as upbeat a tone as I could.

"There's got to be another one, unless you think the hospital never even wrote another one with my birth mom on it."

As Andy was closing the folder, I saw something written at the bottom on a tiny yellow sticky note in light pencil.

Call Angela.

39. Hope on a Post-It Note

Andy's face was lit up and concerned at the same time. It was hard to describe, but his look went from sunshine to dark clouds in seconds. "What do you think it means? Is that her name? Angela?"

It took me a moment to focus. "I have no idea." I was as confused as Andy, and I didn't want him to get his hopes up.

He sat up and began to flip through all the papers stacked around the adoption box. "Her name must be somewhere else in all this stuff," Andy was muttering to himself. But then he stopped and looked right at me.

"Grace, I know I must seem crazy to you. But when my mom talks to me, I can see … I can feel that she loves me, and I don't want to ruin the relationship I have."

"It's not much of a relationship if you can't tell her things and be honest with her."

Andy simply did not appreciate my wisdom. He was preoccupied with his mom's reactions. I tried one more time.

"Trust me Andy, your mom would be okay with all this."

"Forget it, Grace," he snapped.

Oh, well, a sentence too far.

"I am trying to find out WHO. I. AM. Everyone thinks that being adopted happened when I was a baby."

"Well, didn't it?" I asked.

He smacked the box of paperwork. "Yes, the papers were all signed then, but adopted is something that I am and will be for the rest of my life. It's always with me and I'm trying to figure out how it happened. You know your story. I want to know mine."

"That's fair."

"I've been told that I am lucky by millions of people." Andy's voice got high and a little scary. "Oh, you are so lucky to have been adopted by Beth and Tom. What a great family you have."

Then he returned to his own voice that was intensely sad. "What do they know? Do they know what it feels like to be rejected by a mother?

"You don't know that for sure, Andy."

"Yes, I do. I'm sitting here, aren't I? They've put off talking to me like a gazillion times. But honestly, I haven't told them how incredibly important this is to me."

"Well, you could tell them now."

It was clear, Andy did not want to discuss getting his parents in on the KISSS action.

"The adoption agency name is right here at the top of the home study report. It's a Chicago address. Why don't I go home and do a few searches about the agency? We could plan a trip there if you think that's necessary."

"Necessary?" Andy smiled, pumped his fist and jumped up, almost hitting his head on his mom's designer bags that were poking out from the shelves. "Let's go!"

40. Letter to Grammy

It had been a while since I wrote to Mildred. After the closet KISSS meeting with Andy, I decided to write to the most wonderful old person in my life. Not that I didn't appreciate what Mildred had done for me, but Grammy knew me.

> *Dear Grammy,*
>
> *Hello and how are you doing? I hope you like the photo of me in my riding gear. The lessons are fun. My horse's name is Twiggy. Chris is our instructor, and she said Twiggy was perfect for me since we both have long legs. Right now, in class we are mostly walking and trotting. I'm getting better at posting with every lesson.*
>
> *Sometimes when Twiggy canters, I feel a bit off balance and hold on as tight as I can. No spills yet. Thank you so much for taking me shopping and telling Mom that I should have lessons.*

The boy that I know in my riding lesson is Andy, and we are sort of friends. He has asked me to keep a secret for him but it's nothing bad. Still, I don't like keeping secrets. So, do you think it's okay to keep the secret for a little while until he trusts me more? I still don't have many friends so I'm not sure what to do.

Did you ever keep a secret from Mom? Write back when you can.

Your favorite (and only) granddaughter,

Grace Elizabeth

PS: Unfortunately, I still have not mastered the chain stitch. I hope I see you soon for another lesson.

41. Sunday-Not in Church

"So, have you given any thought to the next steps? I was thinking that we could take a trip to Chicago to the adoption agency that my parents used."

Andy had called my cell. I didn't even know he had my number. I was sitting on my bed with Lily bear reading when I picked up. He caught me by surprise. "Oh, wow Andy, I'm not sure we can manage that."

"Grace, you're the one who suggested it. Mom and Dad have taken me into the city a few times, so I think I know my way around."

"And what would we do once we get there?"

"We would go to the agency. It's called Choices Adoption Agency, and I recognize the address. It's on one of the main streets in town, and I know how to get there."

I stared at my phone. KISSS was becoming very real.

42. Friendship is Complicated

Mr. J was his dynamo self when class started on Monday. "Alright." He was trying to get our attention. "Remember, your preliminary essays about family traditions are due on Wednesday. That way, I'll have time to grade and return them by Friday. This is good practice for your full Fall essay, which is due on December fifteenth."

Mr. J seemed extra pumped to give us this news. He was wearing his usual khaki uniform, but I noticed that today he had on colorful crazy socks. They were navy with a burnt orange design, which I knew immediately were Chicago Bears' colors. Football socks are one of my dad's favorite things, and I can spot them a mile away. When he wasn't watching the Eagles, Dad rooted for Chicago. He said that even being a part-time fan helps him feel a part of his new city. Dad's Philadelphia socks are green and black with eagles flying on them. Last Christmas, he bought Nate the same socks. Father and son are insanely close in their football huddle—it's hard to get in sometimes.

My family tradition essay was finished ages ago. It was only three hundred words, the max. Who couldn't write that?

But then Mr. J reminded us that we will need to hand in our topic and outlines for the Fall essay contest before Thanksgiving. What am I going to write about? We had to pick from one of the topics on Mr. J's list or come up with our own. After looking at the list again, I debated between "the importance of kindness" and "the meaning of friendship."

Charlotte came up to me after class and was curious about what I would write. She narrowed it down to the exact same two topics!

"I can't believe we're both thinking about these two," she said. Charlotte's hair was pulled back with clips, but no matter what she did to it, I'm sure all the boys thought she was gorgeous. She was just a tad shorter than me, but then just about everyone was. I knew she had one special friend named Devon because I would see them together sometimes at lunch. Today, Devon and Charlotte came over to sit with Andy and me, and this time Andy seemed to actually like the company.

Conversation was easy, but then Charlotte knocked my socks off.

"Devon is coming over to my house this coming weekend for a sleepover, and we thought it would be fun if you came over too."

On the bus ride home, I couldn't stop thinking about my sleepover invite. It was probably left-over PB&J pity, but I didn't care and had said "Yes!" immediately. My stomach turned itself into a knot wondering if they really wanted to be friends with me or just felt sorry for me. In my head I was jumping up and down. Connie and I had maybe two or three sleepovers. But when our friendship crashed, I never thought it would happen again. The news was big. Did I finally have a friend?

"Mom! Mom, are you home?" I was screaming my head off. Mom came rushing out of the kitchen and I blurted, "Charlotte invited me for a sleepover at her house! We're going to talk about our essays and another friend of hers, Devon, is going to be there too."

"Oh honey, that's great news. I know you have been missing Connie. Who is Devon?"

"She's another friend of Charlotte's. I think they've known each other forever."

"Well, there's nothing like a sleepover for girls to get to know one another. I know you'll have fun."

Even though the sleepover wasn't until the weekend, I pulled out my duffel bag and began to pack a few things. I decided on my favorite pink pajamas plus an old T-shirt and navy sweatpants, because I wanted to be prepared. I didn't want to look like a dork in my pink pj's if casual sweats was a better look.

It also felt like the right time to write THE letter.

Dear Connie,

Thank you for your letters. I am sorry about how things turned out. I understand now that sometimes a friend can get caught in a situation that is not in her control. There's always that chance that things can go too far.

So now I think I finally figured out an important fact about friendship.

I met another girl who is not in my homeroom and her name is Charlotte. We're in the chorus together. Even though I am not very good at it, singing makes me happy. Maybe when you're doing things that you like, it's the best time to meet new people.

Charlotte just invited me to a sleepover, and it made me think of you. But I also have another friend named Andy who I will have to tell you about later. Andy has asked me to help him with a very special project and I'm worried that he'll be disappointed or mad at me.

So, I have decided that friendship is complicated and not always easy to manage.

I know you're happy for me that I am not such a loser. What happens with Andy and Charlotte will be in my next letter, so stay tuned.

Your friend,

Grace Elizabeth

"Gracie, please come down and set the table for dinner. Remember, this is Nate's last week of practice. I carb loaded all our meals this week because he has to stay strong." Mom was trying hard to be cool about it, but I could tell she was one hundred percent invested in doing everything she could for Nate. She took it way too seriously, and sometimes I just wanted to laugh.

"Mom, he hardly even plays."

"Yes, I know, but just in case he needs some extra energy, he'll be ready."

Just then the front door banged open, and it was loud, even for Nate. "Anybody home?"

Mom and I turned the corner to the front hallway and saw Nate. He stood shakily on crutches, leaning up against the door.

43. The Football and Adoption Wound

"Oh, my goodness, what happened?" Mom ran over to Nate and grabbed his backpack. "How did you get here?"

"The coach dropped me off."

She tried to grab one of his arms, but he shook her off and put the crutches back under his armpits.

"Trust me, it's nothing. At least we're at the end of the season and I'll have time to heal. I think I sprained my ankle when I came down after catching an awesome pass at practice today. The trainer put an ACE bandage on it. He told me to elevate and ice it. Dingus, go get me some ice in a plastic bag."

It wasn't the time to give Nate grief. Behind all his ice-it confidence, I could see he was worried.

"Oh, and don't forget a towel."

"Here, let me help you," Mom said as she tried to put her arm around Nate's waist. "I was just telling Grace about our carb-loading strategy."

"Yeah, guess I'm not going to be on the field anytime soon."

Nate sat down at the kitchen table and propped up his foot while I helped arrange the towel and ice. Mom and I finished getting the table and dinner ready and when Dad came home, he heard the whole story again.

"It's already starting to feel better with the ice," Nate said.

It was good for the parents to be distracted. Nate's appetite was also a little off. He wasn't able to shovel the pasta in at the same rate as usual.

Friday came and Andy was there in a flash as soon as I got to homeroom. He had texted me a couple of times last night, but I didn't have time to deal. As soon as I got up to my room, I searched for the Chicago location of Choices Adoption Agency. It turned out that the office was closed on Saturdays, but they had a special adoption book group that met at eleven o'clock. Parents who had applied to the agency and were waiting to adopt had a reading list. It must be crazy waiting to see if you will become a family, and they probably needed something to do.

This month's book was *The Primal Wound* by Nancy Verrier.

I had never heard of a primal wound and immediately looked it up. Turns out that the primal wound is what they think happens when an infant is separated by adoption from the birth mother. The separation causes a primal wound, which can be "traumatic for the child resulting in emotional difficulties."

It's infinitely deep and nothing that you can physically feel in the moment, but later, it makes your heart feel sad and it hurts. Something is missing and you are searching. Is that why Andy was so down in the dumps sometimes?

In my family, I was unhappy for a different reason. I had my roots, so it was nothing like Andy's situation. Nate got all the attention, and that made me bummed out and a bit jealous. But I knew my parents, my story, where I came from, and why I looked the way I did. I was beginning to understand why Andy was bummed out and felt like a part of him had been totally erased ... like it didn't exist. He was desperate to find that link to his past.

The light was beginning to dawn on me about what he wanted from our KISSS. Still, I wasn't sure that I should be the one to help him solve the mystery. One thing was clear though. On Saturday, we'd be heading to Chicago.

44. Football Friday

Charlotte was bouncing up and down in her seat when Andy and I joined her for lunch in the cafeteria. Devon was in line getting some fruit.

"Oh, I can't wait for you to come over on Saturday night. We're going to have loads of fun. Sorry, you're not invited, Andy."

Charlotte said it in a nice way, so I didn't think Andy was offended. Plus, I thought it was good for him to see that I had other friends. At the same time, he knew that we were going to Chicago the next morning for our own adventure.

I was feeling better and better about Charlotte as a potential hanging out friend. On one of the nights before Nate's injury, we were texting all sorts of silly emojis and jokes. Then out of the blue, Charlotte reminded me by text that her essay would be about friendship.

Me too! I was stabbing my phone like Grammy playing solitaire. We had to stop because it was getting late, but I was so giddy knowing we could talk about it later.

Right now, Nate was on my mind. When a member of the family is out of balance, it feels like my whole body is out of whack. How would Mom and Dad react if Nate were seriously injured? Dad and Nate lived and breathed football.

Saturday might be a bad day for me to be out with Andy. Then again, who would miss me? I'd spent most of my fall Saturdays with Andy anyway at our horseback riding lessons. It was cold in the mornings, and we had moved to the indoor arena for our last few lessons. Chris made me promise to come back in the spring for the horse show. Once a year in May at Hawthorne Stables there was a show to celebrate all the classes. Lessons started again in April, so I'd be ready by then.

I remember when Mom announced that Dad would be taking the new job in Chicago. Things seemed out of whack then too. Dad was ultra-moody and constantly traveling back and forth to Chicago. Mom spent more hours than ever looking at her laptop. At one point, I caught her crying. Then the nail biting started again.

Of course, whenever I was out of balance, I wrote to Mildred, Grammy, or any one of the other seniors picked at random. In asking them a bunch of questions, I often figured things out on my own. It also helped when I heard from Connie again.

Andy didn't seem to care at all about the fun I was going to have with Charlotte and Devon at our sleepover since it was happening Saturday night. Still, he stayed with us at the lunch table as we made plans about what ice cream and snacks Charlotte's mom would buy.

"Oh, I bet my mom will want to talk to your mom first," I said. "It's no big deal."

"Sure," Charlotte said as we all gathered up our things. The late bell had already rung.

Mr. J was his usual upbeat and loud self.

"Okay, monsters," he said. "You should have already picked your topic for the essay that's due on the 15th. But I'll need your title and subject by the day before Thanksgiving."

Everybody groaned.

"You've known the schedule for a few weeks, so no complaining."

My friendship topic was solid. Knowing that Charlotte would choose the same topic in boosted my confidence. We could certainly talk about it this weekend. I made a few notes on my outline before going to my next class. Thank goodness it was study hall. After that was chorus—at least the week would end on a good note!

45. The Plan

The Friday night football game was just not as exciting with Nate out of uniform and on the bench. Even though he was pretending that everything was okay, I knew it wasn't. The team had a tough loss. Everyone and everything seemed out of sync.

When he woke up Saturday morning Nate's ankle was still throbbing and he hadn't slept much. Mom and Dad huddled at breakfast to decide what to do next. From her office, I could hear Mom typing away, then she went running into Nate's bedroom.

"Nate, it's time to get moving. I just made an appointment at an urgent care center. The closest one with an X-ray machine is about thirty minutes away."

I certainly didn't want anything bad to happen for Nate, but it was perfect that everyone was so preoccupied and not concerned about me at all.

Wait—that's what usually happened.

I was too self-sufficient for my own good. Well, at least I was using that energy to help a friend. It was the right thing to do.

Trying to be casual about it all, I said, "Andy wants me over at his house today for some school stuff." Mom was hurrying out the door, and I didn't want any thoughts lingering about where I was going to be today.

"Okay." She was distracted and getting her reading material ready for the waiting room. "There is probably going to be a long wait for an X-ray. I assume Saturdays can be very busy at that office."

Dad was already waiting in the car. Mom held the door for Nate as he hobbled out of the house. "Stay out of trouble, dingus," he said out of the side of his mouth.

"I won't."

"Text me and let me know where you are," Mom said.

"I'm just going to ride my bike over to Andy's. We may work on our essays."

As soon as the fam was out of sight, I texted Andy about timing. He was waiting for me at the garage, but when I started to get off my bike and walk it into the garage, he waved me away.

"Grace, remember you said that we would work on our essays at your house." He started making funny faces and moving his head in the direction of his father, who was just coming out of the house. Andy made a quick introduction, not looking at either of us. "Chill," I thought.

"Well, hello, Grace. I've heard so much about you. What are you two up to on this glorious sunny Saturday?"

"It's nice to meet you, Mr. Cassidy. Just boring schoolwork, honestly."

Mr. Cassidy was dressed in Saturday style black athletic pants, a matching zip up jacket and Nike shoes. His sandy brown hair was perfectly styled in a laid back but natural way. I ignored Andy and put my bike in his garage anyway. "Let's go inside and look at our essays. I brought over my rough draft."

Andy already seemed annoyed at me, but I explained once we were out of parental earshot.

"The adoption office is closed 'til eleven o'clock when the book group arrives for discussion. We can't get there too early. I've looked all this up already. Just cool your pits."

"My pits are just fine, thank you. I wanted to get there early."

"Well, we can't be walking around the streets of Chicago like two lost losers. We need a destination. We need a plan. Plus, do you have money for the 'L' pass?"

"Yes, I have some smaller bills for the machine."

We chilled in Andy's basement for a bit to plan our route. While Andy's parents were absorbed in some discussion and breakfast clean up, we made our way to the garage.

"Thank you for having me, Mrs. Cassidy," I said sweetly, halfway out the door. No point in delaying now. It was after ten.

"Oh, that was quick, Grace. Come back when you can spend some more time."

Andy decided to establish the game day plan. "We're going to be riding around for a while, then going over to Grace's house. She has her laptop there, and we may do more schoolwork or just watch a movie."

"Okay, sounds good. Tell your mom I said hi."

"Will do," I squeaked.

It felt funny sneaking out like that under false pretenses, but once we were laughed at by the agency, I was sure that Andy would come clean to his parents, and they would figure this out together. That was my plan, anyway.

You know what they say about plans.

46. Chicago

We rode to the 'L' stop and locked up our bikes at the station. Andy paid for the passes, but then looked confused.

"I've only taken the train a few times. I don't even know where to get off."

"Don't worry, I was just on the train with my Grammy when she bought my riding clothes, so I know the way."

Andy was already sweating.

After my card beeped through the turnstile, I tried to be as confident as I could. "It's the last stop. I looked up everything on Google Maps. We can use my phone if we get turned around."

"I can't even think right now." Andy's hand was shaking as he put his transit card back in his wallet. It didn't help that everything was ear-splitting loud as the train pulled into the station. We settled into seats by the door because he needed as much air as he could get. I think we got a few strange looks, but that could just be me. Finally, the doors closed, and we were on our way.

I took a deep breath. "Well, Andy, the only thing you need to think about right now is, do you know what you're going to say once we get there?"

"Honestly, I haven't thought about it until right now. Maybe I was too scared to."

So much for all our KISSS prep. "What happened to 'This is the most important thing in my life right now'?"

"I mean, I sorta know what I want to say. It's just not sounding perfect in my head."

Lucky for us, the office was a standalone building and not a huge office complex with a million security guards. I could see the sign clearly next to the front door: Choices Adoption. Someone at the reception desk could see us standing on the other side of the glass and buzzed us in. A brown plastic nameplate on the desk said WELCOME.

"Hello, my name is Janice, and I am one of the social workers here. Are your parents here as part of the book group discussion?"

I could hear voices down the hall. Because Andy had no response, the dead silence was awkward. He just stood there staring, mesmerized by the bulletin board behind her. It was a huge cork panel with dozens of photos of adults and children of all ages, shapes, sizes, and colors. Some with single parents, some with two moms or two dads. Most of them seemed to have babies and some had multiple kids. I elbowed Andy. On the wall above it was a handmade sign that read "Our Families" with pink and blue hearts on either side. Balloons cut out of construction paper were tacked on the board with pushpins. Andy just stood there staring, and it occurred to me that he was looking for his parents and hoping to see Angela.

"Focus!" I whispered, but Janice heard me of course and smiled.

"Uh, oh, honestly, we are here to ask some questions about my adoption. My name is Andrew Cassidy, and I was wondering if you ever had a birth mother here named Angela?"

Janice paused her paper shuffling and looked intensely at Andy. She was all business one second ago but stopped cold when he asked about his birth mother.

"Okay, let me get a bit of information. Why don't you come over here and sit with me?"

"This is my friend, and I want her to come too."

Janice motioned me over with a smile.

We moved to a corner of the reception area. There were a few blue plastic chairs, a coffee table with a fake green plant on it and an ugly brown tweedy sofa with two cushions.

"I'd like to get a few details first. Do you go by Andy?"

He nodded.

Janice and Andy sat on the sofa, and she turned to face him. I wanted to be next to Andy and took the chair closest to him. He looked like he needed someone to hold his hand, but no, that would be too weird.

"Andy, there are very specific laws about adoption records in Illinois. I'm afraid that I can't release any information to you ... I'm guessing that you are not eighteen yet. Am I right?"

Andy nodded again, but KISSS kicked in. "Yes, but can you at least tell me if this is the agency that my parents used? Do you know them—Beth and Tom Cassidy?"

"I'm afraid that I'm not even able to tell you that. This is really something for you to discuss with your parents. How did you find us?"

"I found a box in their closet and saw your paperwork. I'm just looking for answers on who I am. Is that so hard for everyone to understand?"

"This is what I do every day, Andy, and I know how important this is. So yes, I do understand. Let me ask you a question. Do you think your parents love you?"

"Yes, of course they do." Andy looked down at the mention of his parents.

Janice continued, "Good, I am glad you know that. But you're still here asking these questions, and that's good! You can have both. Your parents' love does not take away your curiosity, your wondering … your sadness … and that's okay."

"I don't want to lose them so I didn't want them to know."

"Well, Andy, guess what? They don't want to lose you either. And if this is important to you, then you need to involve them."

"But they would be incredibly hurt if they knew that I wanted to know her."

"This," Janice said, pointing to the bulletin board, "is all part of your story, and you deserve to know. Choosing an adoption plan for a baby is one of the most difficult decisions a mother can make. It's complicated, emotional, risky, sad, happy and every emotion you can imagine wrapped up in that one decision."

"How is it all those things? How can a mother be sad, happy … why is it risky?"

Janice leaned in a bit and looked like she wanted to grab a textbook because her tone of voice sounded like Ms. Infante. "Once an adoption plan is even mentioned, there are so many other people involved. Even though it's the birth mother's decision, this whole group—relatives, birth father, friends, social workers and more—they all have something to say. They all want to share their opinion. Just like you are adopted for the rest of your life, the birth mother is also someone who thinks about her decision for many years to come."

"That's why it's really important for me to talk to her. I want to find out what she was thinking. Why didn't she want me?"

"That's what I am trying to tell you. If you give your birth mother and your parents a bit of grace, I guarantee your questions will be answered. I am not saying you will understand everything right away. These conversations take time. But I do promise that you will have a much better idea of the situation facing both families. Loving one family is not a betrayal of the other."

Janice then briefly touched Andy's hand. He looked up, but I couldn't see his eyes.

"Remember Andy, conversations with grace will guarantee generous, forgiving, kind and loving hearts."

With that, Andy smiled. "Janice, I don't think I introduced you to my friend, Grace."

47. Caught KISSSing

Andy walked out into the Chicago sunshine and let out a huge breath. "Wasn't she nice?"

"Yes, I loved the way she told you to ask your parents, which is the same thing I've been telling you for weeks." I couldn't resist saying that.

"Yeah, but she also said that the agency recommends that kids know their story. She seemed kinda surprised that we were there at all."

"And now you'll have to tell your parents that you were here, plus snooping in their closet."

"Yeah, I don't know what I'm going to say yet. I guess I have a few days to figure that out."

It was already afternoon. I hadn't been checking my phone but saw a missed call from Mom. Since we were planning to leave soon, I decided not to call back and risk telltale background noise. We'd be home soon enough.

Andy and I decided to celebrate our KISSS adventure by getting hot chocolate. On the way, we walked through the park and saw The Bean. I got super excited.

"Andy, look, it's The Bean!"

"Yeah, I've seen it before."

We had walked another way to the adoption agency and missed it. But then, we saw what looked like a huge, silver jelly bean. I had heard Mom and Dad mention it a few times. We hadn't yet taken a real tourist trek around Chicago. Everyone was always so busy working.

"Yeah, but you didn't see it with me. Let's see who can make the weirdest face in it."

Andy started running toward it. "Bet you I can beat you there."

We ran up to the giant sculpture and started doing crazy dance moves and faces. It was monumental to see our goofy selves reflected back at us. We kept running up to The Bean, then running away, then running back. By the time we had our hot chocolate, it was getting late.

"C'mon, it's time to head back. We don't have enough homework for our parents to believe we were doing legit schoolwork all this time."

We found the 'L' stop again, but the people coming out from the station told us the trains weren't running. Sure enough, when we went to the platform, a message scrolled in red letters.

SERVICE SUSPENDED ...
POLICE ACTIVITY ON TRACKS

"Oh wow, this will screw up our plans big time." I had my phone in my hand and tried to get some news.

Andy was not pleased but put on a brave face. "Let's just chill here and maybe things will open up soon."

We plopped down on benches at the station, but then, in no time, he was up pacing back and forth.

"Now what?" Andy said, putting his hands in his pockets and muttering to himself.

Just then, my mom called again. I held the phone up to Andy. "Should I answer it?"

"No!" he screamed. "I need a second to think."

I wasn't sure what there was to think about. We were two kids stuck in the city and we needed to get home.

We approached a few people at the station, but no one had any additional information.

"Let's go out and see if we can find a police officer. Maybe they know how long the delay will be," I offered. It was late afternoon, and I was starting to worry.

The day had been all about Andy, but I still had something wonderful to look forward to later, and I was smiling on the inside. My sleepover at Charlotte's house would be my first since we moved. I was making friends! It's going to be absolutely delightful—as Grammy would say—to get to know Charlotte and Devon. I wondered if any other girls were invited.

Andy didn't even wait for me, darting up the stairs and out of the station. We walked around for another twenty minutes, but no police were in sight.

"What now?" I asked. We were both getting nervous. "I'm sorry, Andy, I need to call home. Have your parents called you?"

Andy pulled out his phone. "Oh yeah. Gee, as a matter of fact, my dad called while we were running around The Bean."

"Okay, I'm calling my mom now." I took out my phone again and turned away from him.

48. From Bad to Worse

Both Dad and Mr. Cassidy were in the car to pick us up.

"What were you kids thinking?" Dad was looking right at me and although his voice was not very loud, I could tell he was furious. We buckled our seat belts without saying a word. Dad continued to rant. "Do you realize what could have happened?"

I decided not to chime in with any answers and waited until we were closer to home. "Our bikes are at the 'L' stop," I muttered under my breath as quietly as I could.

"Yeah, we figured that. We'll swing by to pick them up now and then we will have a chat when we get home, Grace."

Mr. Cassidy looked like he wanted to add his two cents. We had already come clean with the reason we were in the city at all. It was not the greatest news to share over the phone and when they picked us up Andy and his dad just looked at each other. Nothing much more was said.

Andy mouthed "I'm sorry" in the back seat as we crawled along in Saturday afternoon traffic. For a quick second, I wanted to laugh because it was fantastically awkward to be caught by our parents this way. Andy's conversation was bound to be way worse than mine.

"Bye, Andy." I waved with a pathetic grin. He didn't seem as concerned as I was, and half-smiled at me when he pulled his bike out of the trunk. Mr. Cassidy put his arm around him when they walked into the garage.

As the automatic door lowered, Dad said again, "What were you thinking?"

"I don't know, I was just trying to help. Andy seemed desperate to find his birth mom and he kept pestering me. I told him to talk to his parents, but he didn't listen."

"Gracie, you could have come to us."

Mom came rushing out to meet the car. "Gracie, what were you thinking?"

"Yes, we've been through that. She was only trying to help. But Grace, for such a sensible, smart girl, this made no sense. We are astounded at your lack of judgment."

Suddenly, I was angry too. "Well, you won't even have to look at me tonight, since I'm going to Charlotte's for a sleepover."

"No, you're not going anywhere," Dad said. "Please just go to your room and leave your phone and laptop on the kitchen table."

"What? You're not letting me go to Charlotte's?"

"No, you are grounded until we say otherwise. It's time for you to think about what an embarrassing situation you put us in with Andy's parents."

"Isn't it your fault I'm in this situation to begin with?" I started to cry, just thinking about my one chance for a friendship being flushed right down the toilet.

"How is this our fault, Grace?"

"Dad, you're the reason we are even living in this town. It's because of you and your new, bigger, and fancier job that we're here in this city. I was fine where we were."

Mom was spitting angry words now. "Grace, that's not fair." She crossed her arms, sat back on the sofa, and looked at Dad to give an explanation.

Dad lowered his voice and began. "Grace, career opportunities are difficult decisions. My job in Philadelphia had come to a dead end. I made the best decision for this family. Yes, it's hard to pick up and move, but you, Nate, and your mother have advantages here that were not possible at your old school. Nate will be coached with a college football career in mind. Your school has already recognized your intellectual talents, and you will be starting a new program next semester for gifted students."

With that news, I sat up straight and looked at my dad. His eyes had lines, and he cleared his throat as he continued. "Business was down at my old agency. We had lost a large client."

He paused for a second to grab Mom's hand across the sofa. They smiled at each other. Mom's nails were a blue gray color with not a chip to be seen. I hadn't noticed that she stopped biting them. "Mom was the one that researched this school district. She contacted the principal when she saw that they were looking for experienced library staff. I thought that Chicago would be a good market for me, and so far, so good. And no, we didn't intentionally try to ruin your life. I will do everything I can for my family. It was a rough transition, but I think it's working out. We shall see. There are no guarantees."

"I'm so sorry, Dad. I didn't know."

"Now we need to think about how to make things right with the Cassidy family. Why don't you let your friends know that you will be staying at home this weekend?"

"I am sorry about the drama and was really only trying to help." I filled them in on getting the adoption agency name from Andy's parents' closet. There wasn't much more to say after that. I texted Charlotte to say that we had a family emergency. She would probably be mad at me. I didn't dare call Andy. Mom was waiting for my phone and laptop anyway.

Lily bear and Grammy's blankets were looking like the only company I was going to have that night.

49. Paper and Pen

I must have fallen asleep, because it was dark when I woke up. I could hear the TV on in the family room. The leftovers were on a tray covered in plastic wrap for me on the counter.

Mom came into the kitchen when she heard me rummaging around. "You looked exhausted, so I thought it best to leave you be."

"Thanks, Mom. I am sorry about everything."

The pizza was cold, but I didn't care.

"Are you sure you don't want me to heat that up for you?"

I shook my head and chomped down on a mouthful of pepperoni, cheese, and tomato.

Mom pulled out a chair and cleared her throat. I sensed a heart-to-heart conversation.

"Honey, I know you said that you and Andy were just friends, but when we couldn't find you, I was looking on your desk and saw some note about kissing and Andy's name was next to it. There were several notes in fact. One was on your homework from English class and another kiss note was stuck in the binder with your school notes. When you and Andy were meeting, I am guessing you were doing more than homework? What's going on between you two? Should I be worried about this relationship?"

Mid-swallow, I spit out a laugh.

"What's so funny?"

"No, it's nothing. Andy and I are just friends. The kissing notes you saw were spelled K-I-S-S-S—all caps with three s's. Did you notice? It stands for Kids in Search of Something Secret. Andy wanted us to have a code name for our operation, and that's what I came up with."

"Oh." Mom made a face that was a mix of surprise and disbelief.

"I know, it sounds stupid, like maybe something little kids would do, but Andy was paranoid about anyone finding out what we were doing."

Mom busied herself cleaning up the kitchen and I could tell she was still mad at me, so I moved to leave.

"Gracie, wait."

I turned around to see Mom looking distraught and holding on to the pizza box. I thought she was going to ask me about how sad Andy and I were now that our plans went to hell in a handbasket, as Grammy always says.

Instead, she admonished, "You didn't even ask me about Nate. Don't you want to know what happened and how he is coping?"

Oh, lots to say about that one. Instead, I kept it short and sweet. "Mom, since it's always about Nate in our house, I was bound to hear eventually. Plus, I am sure I will figure it out the next time I see him."

Mom ignored my sibling snark. "The doctor at urgent care has recommended a hard cast. They think he also has a bone chip that they are going to keep an eye on. We have an appointment with an orthopedic surgeon on Monday. The boot is the best we could do until then."

At the mention of his name, Nate limped into the room, "Any snacks for my movie? Done with all the drama, dingus?"

I turned to go and didn't even feel that bad about ignoring him. Was I becoming more like him?

Back upstairs under my mountain of blankets, I grabbed my flashlight. Who needs a computer when you have paper, pens, a marker, and stickers? Earlier, when I texted Charlotte that I couldn't make it, she texted back, "K." My friendship was reduced to a "K."

Dear Mildred,

Well, I promised a report on the KISSS activities, and guess what? Epic fail.

We were able to find our way to the adoption agency, but nothing doing in finding out anything about Andy's birth mother. We thought we had her first name, but we are not even sure of that.

I am in trouble now with no phone, and no way to contact Andy to find out about how it went with his parents. In the meantime, there is a big to do at our house since my brother was hurt at football practice. Mom and Dad are very preoccupied with all that. Without any screen distractions, I am back to reading and writing letters.

Please know that I am thinking of you and hope you have some cozy blankets now that the weather is turning colder. Do you have movie night where you live? Nate and I used to watch funny movies together all the time. It's weird when kids grow up. The family is not as important as it used to be.

Please take care. You can write to me if you want. Let me know if you have broken any rules recently. I have broken close to an infinite number this week, and could use some company.

Your pen pal,

Grace Elizabeth

50. Back at School

Monday came soon enough. Andy made a beeline for me. I was dying to know what his parents said, but we had to wait until lunch to catch up. In the hallway, I could see Charlotte and Devon deep in conversation. I tried to scoot by, but then felt bad because I did owe them an explanation.

Charlotte didn't give me a chance. "Why did you blow us off at the last minute? You said that you would be there."

"Yeah, I know, but Andy and I got into a bit of trouble over the weekend, and my parents wouldn't let me go. They also took my phone and laptop, so I couldn't tell you anything else. I'm really sorry."

"What kind of trouble?"

"Well, it had to do with Andy and a trip to Chicago. It didn't work out the way we wanted it to, and I was grounded. I can tell you more about it later."

"Okay. Well, we don't want to interfere with your busy schedule." Charlotte had one hand on her hip and was clearly done with me at that moment.

I had that same sickening feeling when Connie gave me the heave-ho, and it made me sad. Would I ever have girlfriends that give me a chance to be me or let me explain myself? I was nobody special. I would never be the prettiest girl in the room or the most interesting. But wouldn't it be nice to have a girlfriend who thought I was cool exactly the way I am? How did everyone else do it? The bright side was that I would be pretty good on a deserted island, like that Cast Away movie I saw once with Nate. Although, that wasn't much of a bright side, if I 'm being honest.

Teachers were talking, explaining, and writing on the SMART Board. I didn't hear a thing. Saturday night and Sunday had felt lonely. It was not one of those times when I wanted to be alone. There was no one to call—even if I did have my phone—and nothing but my letters to keep me company. What a loser. School felt like the first day I was that friendless kid from Pennsylvania.

At lunch, Andy and I settled at a corner table in the cafeteria. He was excited to tell me that his parents weren't even that mad. Finally, some good news. We smiled at each other and made some of the same goofy faces we made at The Bean.

"Not even when they found out we snooped in their closet?"

"No, can you believe it? Mom said they couldn't expect me to be honest with them when they've kept things from me. She thought she was doing the right thing by not telling me about my birth mother. She said that she thought it would be easier if I didn't know all the details."

Andy took a breath and looked right at me. He whispered, "She started to cry when I told her about our conversation with Janice. It was right after I told her what Janice said about giving my birth mother some grace."

"Why did she start to cry?"

"Mom said that my birth mother said the exact same thing. Isn't that weird?"

"I don't understand."

"Mom said that when they met my birth mother for the first time, she asked Mom for grace. She just couldn't take care of me and didn't want my mom and dad to judge her."

"What did your mom say?"

Andy stopped to bite into his apple. Lunchtime was almost over, and we had barely touched our food.

"Then my dad stepped in because Mom was still kind of crying and she just wanted to hold my hand. Dad said, 'Without her, we wouldn't have you, so we told her we would give her all the grace that she could handle.'"

"Sounds a lot better than the discussion I had with my parents."

"Mom and Dad both said they were sorry for not listening to me. They convinced themselves it was easier not to tell me stuff but were now realizing they probably just avoided the whole conversation because it was easier for them. Then we had a whole big conversation about everything that happened before the adoption, how it went down, and the whole shebang."

I was genuinely happy for him, and he was grinning ear to ear. When did he start saying shebang?

Andy stood to throw away his lunch trash.

The bell rang and we walked back to our homeroom. Andy was floating just ahead of me.

Before we sat down, Andy yelled to me, "And guess what? Her name is Angela!"

51. Even Andy

Mr. J's class was at least something to look forward to. I was getting my grade today for the holiday traditions essay. Also, I submitted my topic for the fall contest early. Because I had already started working on my friendship essay, I hoped to get the green light today.

Mr. J does not have assigned seats, but we always sit in the same spots. The essays were face down on our desks. I turned mine to the back critique sheet: A. Well, at least that's good news. The holiday tradition I ended up writing about was kind of quirky, but with a bit of family psych thrown in. Mr. J must have liked it. The truth is that beyond church, there is not much we do together as a family, except during the holiday. Nate and Dad talk endlessly about football. The Christmas holiday is time off for Mom, so she does research for a book she's been talking about writing forever. I don't even know what the book will be about.

The time that is the most fun is after Christmas dinner. Nate and I always have a contest at dessert time. It's a game my mom invented called Snowball. You take a large scoop of vanilla ice cream, form it into the shape of a snowball and roll it in coconut. Next, just for decoration, you draw a holly leaf with a food coloring pen and then insert a small birthday candle at the top of the ball. On your mark, get set, go! See who can keep the candle lit the longest while continuing to eat the ice cream. Every year, Nate's candle fizzles out, while mine stays lit, and I win! It's the only thing I can do better than Nate. Of course, I am not counting our writing and book reports.

But maybe I should.

In my essay, "A Snowball's Chance," I explained the game and competing against Mr. Perfection. In the end, it made for a funny story, and obviously Mr. J loved it. I was so busy picturing my report card A that I didn't hear Mr. J calling me over to his desk after class.

"Grace, I loved your essay. Families can be tough during the holidays."

"Yes, but it was a fun topic to write about."

"Actually, I wanted to talk to you about another topic. I have your friendship essay title and outline, and I don't think I can accept it."

"What? Why not? This is the biggest friendship story I have ever had, and I wanted to write about it."

"Yes, but the subject matter is Andy's adoption."

"Oh, I thought that might be a problem, so I changed his name in the essay."

"Grace, I'm sorry, but I just don't think that this is your story to tell. Everyone knows that you and Andy are friends and that you would be talking about him. Andy might not want those details shared."

"Well, I could ask him."

Mr. J stopped for a moment and began shuffling papers and straightening all the weird teacher gifts on his desk … things like a wooden apple and a Smurf doll in school colors. He sat down—it looked like the conversation was over. Then he said in a deeper voice, "Grace, I am not going to approve this outline, and I'd like you to come up with another topic."

With that, he handed back my paper with the note: New outline due Wednesday.

I was staring at the paper and shuffling out of the classroom when Andy came right up to my face.

"I heard everything Mr. J said to you, and I cannot believe that you were going to write about my personal story. Is that what this was to you,

Grace? Just another great essay assignment? I knew you liked to write, but my business is nobody else's business!"

Andy yelled that last line and I stepped back, almost tripping over my own feet. Where was this coming from?

"But, Andy, you've been in this school since you were in kindergarten. I'm sure a lot of kids here know you're adopted."

"Yes, maybe some do, but Mr. J always posts the essays on the school hallway bulletin boards. There are a lot of other kids here who don't know me, and I don't want everyone reading about my biggest secrets."

Truthfully, I didn't even think of that. But I did remember that Mr. J said he would post all our work in the hallway, but not his critique sheet which would include our grade. That made sense.

"Andy, I'm sorry, I thought it was sort of well-known, even though you don't talk about it much. Plus, it's a good story with a happy ending."

"What? Grace, you don't know that! We have just started to talk now about me meeting Angela. Who knows how that will go?"

"Wow. I am sorry. You know I mean it."

"Next time, I think you should consider other people's feelings."

With that, Andy turned and walked down the hallway without even a goodbye.

Mom was still in the library. I thought it would be easier to get a ride home with her and not face anyone on the bus.

"Everything okay, kiddo?" Mom said in a quiet voice, not looking at me because she was busy packing up.

I didn't want to go through the whole story with her, so I just said, "Yeah fine."

52. Grammy Cares

There was one person who would be glad to hear from me. On my bed, I made a desk with a couple pillows plus a big hardback fairy-tale book to lean on.

> *Grammy,*
>
> *What is new with you and when are you coming to see us? I am sorry that I have not asked about your life or kept up with my letter writing. We will have to make time for another crochet lesson when you are here. Or maybe we could do a video lesson. That would be fun, although I'm still not very good with the hook.*
>
> *My riding lessons are over until the spring. I learned so much, and thanks to you, I looked good!*
>
> *The real reason I am writing is that I need someone to talk to. Remember how I told you about a secret that I was keeping? Well, it was*

about my friend Andy. He's adopted and wanted me to help him look for his birth mother.

We secretly found out the name of the adoption agency, then went to Chicago to ask about her. Then I made a mess of everything else.

Andy wanted to keep everything secret, and when Mom and Dad found out what we were doing, it was bad. Plus, I know Mom told you about Nate's football injury. Everyone is very worried about him. I tried to blame Dad for everything, but that was just wrong.

Andy thought I just wanted to use our adventure as an essay topic and now he's mad at me. Mom and Dad are also mad at me for not telling them anything. Later tonight after dinner, I will be telling Nate that I won't be helping him with homework anymore and I guarantee he will be mad at me.

He won't be moving around much with a hard cast on his foot, so he'll have plenty of time for schoolwork.

Do you think things will get better?

Love and hugs from your favorite granddaughter,

Gracie

About the Author

Anna Maria DiDio is an adoptive mother, speaker and author of multiple best-selling children's books. She is a swimmer, quilter, baker and washed-up athlete who is addicted to thin and crispy chocolate chip cookies. She resides in The City of Brotherly Love. Learn more about her at amdidio.com.

More by Anna Maria DiDio

Love at the Border: An Adoption Adventure and Memoir

Many People to Love (L.I.F.E. Adventures #1)

How I Wonder Where You Are (L.I.F.E. Adventures #2)

Carla the Conqueror (L.I.F.E. Adventures #3)

Additional writings on Medium:
medium.com/@annamaria.didio

Made in the USA
Middletown, DE
23 November 2024